Penguin Books
GLANCING BLOWS

Alex Buzo was born in Sydney in 1944, and was educated
at The Armidale School and the University of New South
Wales. He became one of the leaders in a revival of
Australian play-writing, with productions of 'Norm and
Ahmed', 'Rooted', 'The Front Room Boys' and 'The Roy
Murphy Show'. His most recent play, 'The Marginal
Farm', premiered in Melbourne in 1983.

Apart from his play-writing, Alex Buzo has contributed
articles to *The Sydney Morning Herald*, *The Age*, *Pol*,
Playboy, *Reader's Digest*, *Financial Review*, *National
Times*, *Good Weekend* and several literary magazines.
Among his previously-published books are; *Tautology*,
Meet the New Class and a novel, *The Search for Harry
Allway*.

Alex Buzo lives in Sydney with his wife, Merelyn, and
daughters, Emma and Laura. He is an A-grade tennis
player.

For
Valerie Lawson

Alexander Buzo

Glancing Blows

Life and Language in Australia

Illustrations by Ken Hall

Penguin Books

Penguin Books Australia Ltd,
487 Maroondah Highway, P.O. Box 257
Ringwood, Victoria, 3134, Australia
Penguin Books Ltd,
Harmondsworth, Middlesex, England
Viking Penguin Inc.,
40 West 23rd Street, New York, N.Y. 10010, U.S.A.
Penguin Books Canada Limited
2801 John Street, Markham, Ontario, Canada, L3R 1B4
Penguin Books (N.Z.) Ltd.
182-190 Wairau Road, Auckland 10, New Zealand

First published 1987 by Penguin Books Australia.

Typeset in Century Expanded and Helvetica Condensed by Leader Composition Pty. Ltd.
Made and printed in Australia by Australian Print Group

Buzo, Alexander, 1944-
Glancing blows.

ISBN 0 14 009725 2.

I. Hall, Ken. II. Title.

A828'.307

Contents

Introduction
Furry Speech

1	Three Decades of Slang	3
2	Jargonauts at Large	11
3	The Freemasonry of Abbreviations	19
4	A Tinnie Ear for Dialogue	20
5	Colloquiala	21
6	Language of the North Queenslanders	22

In Society

7	The End of the New Class	27
8	Meet the Old Class	28
9	Duel of the Decade: Alisons v. Karens	39
10	The Big Whinge	45

Art and Ent

11	Your Complete Television Guard	47
12	Rockley Herbert Writes for You	50
13	The Young Person's Guide to the Theatre: Credits	52
14	Sets for Plays I Never Wrote	53

Local Choler

15	Cremorne: Peninsula of Gentility	63
16	Townsville: Beyond Thunderbox	68
17	The Big Apricot	73
18	The Big Tomato	80
19	Encounters with South Australians	82

Sports

20 The Whole Comp Tennis Catalogue   95
21 Social Cricket Manoeuvres   102
22 Polo Vaulting   113
23 On First Learning that Norths Have Signed Olsen
    Filipaina   116

Results

24 The Grand Mixmasters   119
25 The Last Tautology Pennant   125

Children of Parody

26 The All-comers Puff Contest   137
27 Academia Awards   138
28 Time, After Time   146

Satire Limits

29 Tautology Unbound   151
    Notes on Contributions   153

Furry Speech

1 Three Decades of Slang

The Goodbye Burl

'**S**it back and have a few tubes', urged Fred Stolle on a dry spring night. Fred was one of the commentators for the US Open Tennis telecast on Channel Nine. I am talking, by the way, about the *1985* US Open. It must have been at least twenty years since I last heard bottles of beer referred to as tubes, but then Fred Stolle left Australia around twenty years ago and expatriates always think their homeland stays exactly as it was when they left. One of the chief virtues of expatriates is that they provide a living link with our past. As a collector of dated slang I find their help invaluable.

In the 1950s and early sixties a party was a turn, a cigarette was a durry or a weed and approval of something was expressed by calling it dapper, immaculate or grouse. Grouse was of course very old Australian slang but it made a comeback then, much as daggy has today. In the 1950s only the oldies said daggy. Slang then used to be simple and expressive. A pimple was a choong and a fast drive was a fang. An attractive bird was a good sort and the collective noun for a flock of really nice-looking sheilas was snoo. The highlight of anyone's weekend was to drink a few tubes and have a few pashes. You never heard cigarettes referred to as gaspers or coffin nails.

By the mid-sixties the Age of Innocence was over. Fred Stolle had gone overseas and slang had become a cultural battlefield. There has always existed in Australia a group of men and women who are dedicated to the immediate adoption of American trends. The differences in climate, geography, history and population have ensured that not all American trends have caught on in

Australia. Those who would wish it otherwise had their day in the sixties. Anyone who was into slang could see guys splitting with chicks in the wheels if they had the bread. Of course, they weren't always off to have a groovy rap; on occasions people would freak out or at the very least become spaced out, which was incredible, but it was what was happening if you were with it. For the olds, it was a time to sit back with a strung-out feeling and watch the youthquake do its thing. Those Who Believed in American Trends certainly had their victories in the sixties, but unfortunately many of them became addicted to smack and then snuffed it. A defiantly colloquial Australian theatre was born around this time and proved something of an irritation to the Yankophiles, who went off to the movies instead. One legacy of this attempted American invasion is the seemingly perennial guys versus blokes division. Australians remain split right down the middle about whether a chap is a guy or a bloke. All we need now is for cove or coot to follow in the wake of grouse and daggy and make a comeback. That could really throw a Sidchrome in the Honeywell.

Quiet Days in Cliché: The Museum of Catch-Phrases

The student of language will more than likely become awestruck when contemplating the rise and fall of catch-phrases. Where did they come from? What accounted for their popularity? Where are they now? Perhaps we can make a tentative start by examining those catch-phrases that came from entertainment. Fairly obviously, most are associated with famous entertainers: 'Strike me lucky', 'How sweet it is', 'Bring your money with you', 'I am the greatest', 'Hi-ho everybody', 'Men 'n' women 'f 'stralia', 'Book him, Danno', 'Hidey-hodey everyboady', 'ET phone home', 'I'm sorry, he's from Barcelona', 'Missed it by that much', 'Rick a pooty and a-fandoogly', 'Do yourself a favour', 'I love your faces'. Equally obvious, I think, is the fact that these entertainers stuck some chord with the public, but then their phrases became interred with them when the inevitable happened and the coiner lost favour with those who repeat catch-phrases.

Other exhibits in the museum should inspire awe, such as

'What do you think this is, bush week?' I never heard this question answered, probably because no one knows what constitutes 'bush week'. Another catch-phrase that has broken many records for longevity is 'Winners can smile and losers can please themselves'. I have never known what this means.

Some of the mustier entries are those with a libertarian flavour. The cobwebs are now very thick on 'Get your gear off', 'Don't do anything I wouldn't do', 'I wouldn't crawl past her to get to you', 'It doesn't matter where you put it as long as it disappears' and 'Ohr would I love to!' Even the only very faintly salacious 'Where do you get it?' seems to invoke a world that has gone.

Among contemporary catch-phrases 'flavour of the month' is flavour of the month. Perhaps I am letting my heart run away with my head but I would not like to bet on its lasting. On the other hand I wish a long life and a merry to 'You'll just have to cop it sweet' and 'X is not impressed'.

If I sound unwilling to ascribe origins and motives for the popularity of catch-phrases, then it could be that I have had my fingers burned, and thus encumbered, have not come out smoking. Those who set themselves up as experts in linguistic matters are often brought down with a bang, a thud, or a vengeance. I recall with horror the occasions I have said that, in Australia, basin is not pronounced bison, and all those tired old jokes about washing your face in an elk just aren't accurate enough to be funny. I got my come-uppance in a bakery in Armidale, New South Wales. I asked the girl behind the counter if they had any damper-style bread. She was most indignant. She glared at me and said, 'We don't sell stale bread'.

Fashions in Sports Language

There is one group of people in our society who are almost completely the victims of fashion. As soon as a new word or phrase is in vogue they all take it up with shrieks of joy. Fads and fancies are their life and they'd never be caught dead using an outmoded expression. I refer to sports commentators.

When I was growing up a bumper in cricket was a short-pitched delivery. But now simply *no* one says bumper. They all say bouncer or, in the case of Tony Greig, short-pitched delivery. Similarly, the wonderfully ominous-sounding googly has disappeared. Anyone who says googly now will find people examining them for traces of exhumation. The correct term is wrong 'un. Any sports commentator worth his salt would simply never *dream* of referring to a high kick in rugby league as an up-and-under. The 1980s fashion is to describe it as a bomb. In tennis, too, the fashion-conscious refer to a googly serve as a kicker, whereas it used to be the American Twist. Perhaps this is some kind of retaliation for the dropping of Australia Crawl in favour of freestyle in swimming. The kicker, like the wrong 'un, bounces the opposite way from that which is expected. This used to require putting *spin* on the ball. Now it is more fashionable to say 'That had a lot of *work* on it.' If you hear someone say toss instead of lob then the sensible thing to do is ring the museum immediately.

In football, a player used to be guilty of dropping the ball. Now he coughs up the football. It was veteran coach Jack Gibson who started the vogue for saying the football instead of the ball. There is something strangely persuasive about Black Jack and pretty soon all the other media worthies followed suit. If you call it a cod or a goolie then you are someting out of a time capsule.

Australia won the Davis Cup in 1983 and the effect on language was immediate. Pat Cash paid public tribute to his team-mates when he said, 'The guys played tremendous, they played unbelievable.' From then on at every level guys were playing tremendous or unbelievable. The tennis fraternity even today uses the adverb very sparing. Has sports language changed for the better or worse? One point to keep in mind is that, as with Melbourne's weather, if you haven't got a big rap on what it's like now, just wait for an hour and it'll be a different ball-game.

Old Slang Time

For some people it's old china, for others old musicals; some collect biographies of Spangler Arlington Brugh, while others hoard New Caledonian postage stamps or show you the pipes they shoplifted in 1959. We all know the buffs who've got all but one of the skis used by F. D. Roosevelt during his first visit to Yalta in that fateful summer of '42 and we all marvel at their yellowing but unbroken sequence of *Newsweek* and *Proceedings: The Journal of the Institute of Civil Engineers.*

But for me it's different. For me, it's old slang. I kind of get a kick out of it and hell, who cares if most of it is American *and* illiterate to boot? Who needs all those warped Kalin Twins records when you've got slang to help you remember?

Let us look at three decades of old slang, all of it now dead, and see if we can share in collectors' items that belong to everybody.

1950s (1955–63)
brass — money

dibs — marbles

turn — party

pash — kiss

hurve — hurry, e.g. I'll hurve back to my place and get some brass.

fang — drive fast, e.g. We went for a fang along the Wakehurst Parkway.

oldies — parents

weed — cigarette (in the city)

durry — cigarette (in the country)

choong — pimple, e.g. Don't pop your choongs in here.

rude — substandard, e.g. These Viscounts are a rude weed.

norks — breasts

grouse — satisfying

strides — trousers. Another one that came back.

see you round — goodbye

hidey-hoady everyboady — no precise definition can be given for this.

dapper — expression of approval for item of clothing, e.g. Those shoes are bloody dapper.

what are you? — all-purpose query

horrid — not meeting expectations

log — sluggish, oafish footballer

toe — pace, speed

flip — mentally unstable person

flog — foolish person

flying feature — brief but dynamic appearance

kewah kewah kewah! — swimming coach's exhortation

Ocker — someone called O'Connor

cacky-hander — southpaw

nut-chokers — (tight) underpants

bug rake — comb

snot rag — handkerchief

dad — originally daddio, an exotic person wearing suede shoes. More generally, it meant 'mate'. Popularised by television show '77 Sunset Strip'. For a time it was used to punctuate *every* sentence.

turps — beer

massive — good

keen — good

fantabulous — good

extra good — massive

gas — good

king — massively good, exceeding all expectations

immaculate — profoundly satisfying

cod — ball. It was the fashion for footballers to yell out 'My cod! My cod!' when they were about to take a high ball.

cat — footballer who yelled out 'Your cod!'

old tart — slow cat

log cabin — dressing-room of the North Sydney Rugby League team in a lean year

This is unfortunate — public relations person's response to disaster

Dialogue clichés of the period included: 'Why not? They say everyone has a double', 'I got the holy man stashed in back' and 'I won't tell Mr Kent if you don't, Miss Lane'.

1960s (1964–71)

Into — involved with, enthusiastic about

unreal — agreeable

split — leave

chick — girl

boobs — breasts
wheels — car
incredible — all-purpose no-meaning word
peace — hello or goodbye
bread — money
freak out — express dismay or shock, either voluntarily or involuntarily
rap — talk warmly, agree on everything
groovy — good
right on — I agree
no risk — general rhetorical affirmative response
crash-hot — good
ciao — goodbye
cool — in full command of one's faculties and social position
roadie — road manager
man — replacement for 'dad'
scungy — unattractive, seedy
naff — scungy
shack up — live with
spaced out — reeling
strung out — reeled
peoples — everyboady
Tumbarumba — country town; floor-shaking dance
teach-in — long rap
relevant — immune from criticism
olds — parents
Ocker — someone who looks as if he should be called O'Connor
southpaw — left-hander
awee-oo awee-oo awee-oo — swimming coach's exhortation
nice girl, but . . . — a female foible has been detected
experimental — immune from understanding
crucial — something that should be agreed with
break-through — something that must be agreed with
This is incredible — public relations person's response to disaster
where it's at — centre of progressive thought
it's what's happening — decentralised progressive thought
roach — smallest viable unit of marijuana
with it — unashamedly contemporary in outlook
now generation — young people

youthquake — display of friskiness by members of the now generation

switched on — with it

heist movie — film in which robbery features (e.g. *The Big Snatch*)

snuff movie — film in which suicide features (e.g. *The Big Hatch*)

Dialogue clichés of the period included 'Take these thongs down to forensic' and 'We blew it'.

1970s (1972–79)

crumblies — parents

slack — mediocre, tardy, apathetic

trendy — fashionable, with special reference to white-wine drinkers

wank — work of art in which self-indulgence is in the eye of the beholder

unbelievable — massively incredible

update — learn latest news, spend more money

line ball — close decision; expression which enables pundits to sound precise while failing to commit themselves

right, right — I agree; I'm still listening; You poor kid

bouncer — bumper

put-down — insult

cop-out — change from one pressure group to another

ego-trip — excessive display of ambition

come-on — excessive display of friendliness

get your act together — terminate period of slackness

up front — failure to conceal motives; brash display of sincerity

no way — unequivocal rejection

one-off — I'll be lucky to get away with this

consciousness-raising — awareness-producing

ongoing dialogue — viable rapport

hype — excessive promotion

grotty — distasteful

the too-hard basket — the task confronting Hamlet

slowmo — action replay

informational — propagandist

semiotics — signs or symptoms arranged in highly subjective manner

stereotype — satirical figure which is close to the bone

wheels — running shoes

bake — criticise trenchantly

tacit endorsement — votes arranged in a highly subjective manner

Turps — quiz compere Ian Turpie

kwah kwah kwah! — swimming coach's exhortation

Ocker — someone called Hogan

dead-set — fair dinkum

left-hander — American champion

What's your story? — half-hearted enquiry into motivation

This is unfortunate — public relations person's response to disaster

definitive — something you agree with

good one — let's change the subject

guidelines, womanspeak, childshock, lifestyle, Zeitgeist — flagships of a successful German invasion

oral history — old slang

Okker — Dutch tennis player

Dialogue cliches of the seventies included 'Maybe they want us to think that, Danno' and 'I won't tell Mr Kent if you don't, Miss Lane'.

2 Jargonauts at Large

If slang is something to cherish, then on the other side of the moon it's hard to feel the same about jargon. Yet, as with slang, many see jargon as a perfectly justifiable, even imaginative, departure from the norm. One thing is certain, however: the jargonauts are here to stay, rather than being in a transitory one-off situation on the back burner, as they would say with here's-your-hat frankness.

Sports

As long as temperamental stars are prepared to shed their 'bad boy' tag, as long as Norman May keeps saying things like, 'It was a dead heat between Azeem and the ball with the ball just winning', there will always be sports jargon. Rex Mossop cemented a spot as doyen of the breed in two of his planned set-piece moves from the Rexicon: 'Canterbury ceased to be a cohersive force', and 'They've been going on and on about it *ad nauseam* — that means forever'.

Critiques

Some of the strident voices from the left and right have toned down in the post-Tynan era. If a leftie wants to rubbish a work which fails to please then it will be seen as lacking vision or not politically challenging. Meanwhile, over on the right, any effort with a remotely pinkish tinge will be condemned as dogmatic. The characterisation in any suspected left-wing narrative is never believable. There are some constants, however. Everything from Sydney is superficial while even the most threadbare tour by the Royal Shakespeare Company has sets that are stunning. Rising above the ruck, the definitive voice must surely belong to Ian Robinson: 'Sandy Gore made Alex Buzo's *Coralie Lansdowne* her own in a quite unique way'.

A heightened sense of *déjà vu* was provided in 1986 [sic] by South Australian theatre critic Bob Evans, who wrote a paean to *Hedda Gabler* in the *Sydney Morning Herald*. He was most taken with Hedda's pistols and said of them: 'It is typical of the irony of Ibsen's imagery that he uses a phallic symbol to represent the impotence of Norway's upper classes'.

John Cargher laid a claim to equal uniqueness among critical jargonauts when he wrote in *Music for Pleasure*: 'Jean Sibelius (1865–1957), on the other hand, is a true giant among composers, though he also was a unique one-only figure in the musical life of an otherwise musically barren country, Finland'. Oh, well. As one critic said, 'It's a cyclical thing that ebbs and flows'.

Age Rage

Forget all about your links and leaks. They're just too green on their own without a bit of age. Popular usage now demands linkage, leakage, stoppage, haulage, yardage (metreage?) and signage. Yes, signage. A spokesperson for the Department of Main Roads was describing the lack of anticipatory visual material on one highway. 'The signage is poor', he said. I'm waiting for him to assist some far-flung graziers to convert from gates to ramps. After the rampage there would, presumably, be less lossage of stock and few stampedes.

Concern Going

As far as I'm concerned ... this used to be a perfectly grammatical cliché. But now, in this uncaring age, we seem to have lost concern. 'As far as' is all they say and the rest is silent. 'As far as the future is concerned, well, that of course depends on what happens', said National MLA Leon Punch, but he was part of a dwindling minority. 'As far as the ACTU', 'as far as the government', 'as far as Darwin', all over, in fact, the concern was understood.

Flogged

Political jargon has been content to deal in routine horrors like grandfather clause and preferred option. Perhaps the most disappointing failure was the home-spun rhetoric of Senator Flo Bjelke-Petersen during the 1984 campaign: 'In New South Wales under Wran they've been ransacked; in Victoria under Cain they've been caned; and in Canberra under Hawke they've been ... they've had a lot of ... uh ... problems ...'.

Ing Dynasty

Before anyone could say 'knifing' the Ing Dynasty was

entrenched. We had funding, bruising, backing, pricing, logging and polling. In the bathroom you could find towelling. But the Ing Dynasty are not arrogant spouting people. Most of them are grateful if over their heads they've got roofing. And around the house? Fencing or hedging is all the go, with gating or ramping for those in the bush. Dooring and sinking come later.

Television Capsules

'A predictable saga featuring the ever-popular canine' was one description of a Lassie film. A leading TV guide described *Ali Baba* as a 'costume actioner'. Those who write about television experience many highs and lows. From joyous outings and satisfying fare through mixed entries and off-beat oaters they can plunge to atrocious farce and uninteresting melodrama. 'That's been the tale of Australia's story today', said Darrell Eastlake, and that just about sums up the précis. Occasionally, however, exhaustion sets in and the television writers play it tight. For sheer economy I love this off-beat entry:

Jason and the Argonauts (63, Rpt.)
Adventure based on the Ancient Greek legend
Starring Todd Armstrong and Nancy Kovack

Journalism

Many journalists cannot help themselves when it comes to beginning articles with 'Andy Warhol once said that in the future everyone will be famous for fifteen minutes' despite the saying's patent falsity. This *is* the future and no one has been famous for fifteen minutes (with the possible exception of Todd Armstrong and Nancy Kovack), yet many journalists are denied the kind of therapy that would prevent them from beginning their articles with this hollow chestnut.

And Racism

In the seventies many New Class people chose to end their sentences with 'and racism'. This is not to be confused with Ayn

Randism, which is a hearse of a different colour. Many bogus New Class causes were bolstered by tacking on 'and racism' and all sorts of innocent Old Class people found themselves accused of racism, just as many bogus Old Class causes have been justified by Ayn Randism. They include many cost-cutting measures undertaken by governments in the name of self-sufficiency and Reaganism.

Sex in the Eighties

No such thing, I'm afraid. In a lightning coup it was replaced by gender. Regardless of gender, regardless of gender became an instant cliché, as did gender gap, which is admittedly better than sex shortfall. In an ironic appropriation of the enemy's language, some Old Class males began to protest about 'gender fascism' as the Affirmative Actionettes threatened their jobs.

Today8s Specials

That was what I saw chalked on a blackboard at a New York tavern where writers used to go. Every writer has hit 8 instead of its neighbouring apostrophe when typing. But to write it out in chalk? I thought it was the best and funniest sign I'd ever seen, and so did the New York writer who took me to the tavern, once I'd explained it to him.

Tense Gripping

'The trouble with you, Buzo, is that you have mixamatensis,' said B.J. Mattingley, my English master at school. Indeed, I always have had, slipping from present tense to past and then I go back again. Mixamatensis is widespread in Australia ('I grabbed Bluey and he's hit me with the poker and down I went') and is often used to good narrative effect. Many a yarn-spinner switches to the present tense and has thereby heightened the drama. I think it has been perfectly legitimate and will continue to be.

Sign Age

A sign outside the Capitol Cinema in Armidale reads, 'This theatre has been closed due to the absorbtion of its egress by the Dumaresq Shire Council'. Once upon a time the jargon of the bureaucracy was kept behind closed doors. Now its cockatoos have gone out into the community and spread the good word. Before we examine this impact, let us consider the quality of bureaucratese. The fateful sign that announced the closure of my childhood palace of dreams will do nicely.

First, the Capitol shows films and is thus a cinema, not a theatre. Towards the end of its days the Capitol forswore films in favour of major motion pictures but this still did not make it a theatre. Second, every time I see due to I feel the crash of BJM's ruler on the desk. Not due to, the expression is owing to! Absorption was spelt with two bees and the choice of egress was surely unfortunate. Apart from that, I thought it a wonderful sign, in the great tradition of 'Go back. You are going the wrong way' and 'Falling Rocks Do Not Stop'.

Cockatoos of the Bureaucracy

Those who saw it will not forget the appearance on television of a spokesperson for Police-Citizens Clubs. 'The whole approach of our organisation', promised the bureaucrat, 'will be non-sexical'. Not to be outdone, the University of Singapore took us back further than the 1970s when it advertised for a job that carried with it the promise of monthly emoluments. Members of the Australian Writers' Guild were startled by one definition of their status by a television executive. He described writers as 'the software supply side of the industry', a wonderfully permanent-sounding definition for the average scribe who struggles for media feedback or tries to establish shelf credibility. Unfortunately for those who work in television, however, the funding situation is such that funding is in a situation where there is a question mark over the funding situation.

End Game

We have seen the kind of expertise that bureaucrats bring to their use of the language. What, then, is the result when these cockatoos broadcast their message to an eager world? Well, to put it simply, the multi-factorial self-actualising randomisation of fast-lane promotorial approaches has led to the accelerated acculturation of human-intensive infrastructures in quotidian one-one-one empathy situations to the point where, in effective terms, the unbottomable input of decelerated routinisation is in turnaround and unlikely to impact on demographic force-fields of a conurbanic kind. Or whatever. Those who would like a translation of that are urged to be patient. Those who would like the cockatoos of the bureaucracy to return to their cages have my support.

Hoi!

One of the few indicators of social class in Australia is hoi polloi. When used correctly, i.e. to mean the rabble, it indicates that the user is part of the educated middle class. When used incorrectly, i.e. to mean the educated middle class, it indicates that the user is from the hoi polloi.

Jargon Abroad

'It was ossom. It was slotter', said Tony Trabert of a one-sided tennis match. Where would we be without American commentators? Without commentators, probably. Bjorn Borg works for CBS as a contributing analyst. He is still, however, an ice-cool Swede. Some things never change, and Wimbledon has always been replete with dour Czechs, volatile Ecuadorians and little-known Queenslanders. Maybe it's the strobberries.

Big City

In the beginning there was ethnicity. Then historicity. The
architects of the new Dickensian age just couldn't help making
extensions. Ethnocentricity. The biggest horror of all was
specificity, Bob Hawke's favourite. I suspect he only used it to
show he was still on mineral water.

Old Feller My Country

Percy Grainger is dead. It will be for his efforts in music
composition rather than language that he will be remembered, I
feel. As a linguist, Grainger was all for purging English of any
Latin or Greek roots. He declared himself in favour of a Kipling-
style 'blue-eyed English' and suggested replacing democracy
with chance-for-all-y and critic with weight-worth. Unfortunately he would have suffered most under the Newkspeak
regime, with the Latinate Percy probably being replaced by
Stalky and Co.

Foon Sped

Some of the most famous spoonerisms over the years have been
newts on the nose and blushing crow. Footballer Peter Sterling
took the spoonerism into new territory when he tried to express
gratitude to his sponsor for an award on live television. What he
meant to say was 'I'd like to thank Winfield . . .'.

Foot Loose

The resignation of Liberal Rosemary Foot from the Bear Pit
(NSW Parliament) prompted a couple of jargonauts into action.
Mrs Foot's putative replacements included one who was a
pragmatic dry (i.e. right-wing) and another who was thought to
be a captive of the uglies (i.e. right-wing). Although no one said
it, the implications were that Mrs Foot was damp and beautiful,

woolly and liberated. In the world of jargon, at least there is freedom of choice.

3   The Freemasonry of Abbreviations

When I started out in the theatre I had to learn the special language of abbreviations of my new occupation. Most areas of work have their own freemasonry and when you learn to use this code then it usually means that you have arrived or you are unimaginative, or both.

'That's very g.p. but it's not g.p. enough for the Madge. Try the Toot', a head mech told me about an early play of mine. G.p. means general public and a play that is g.p. is commercial and can expect good b.o. (or box office). The Madge was Her Majesty's Theatre while the Toot was the Old Tote Theatre. Mech was short for mechanist, or scene-shifter, and if you were head mech for JCWs you were at the peak of g.p. theatre, which in those days was run by the spiritual descendants of James Cassius Williamson. I also learned that stage right was the OP side, being opposite the prompter, and that the tech came before the dress otherwise it was NBG. Of course, in those innocent times you could put on a show without worrying whether it was IUS or not. There were no worries about being ideologically unsound.

In journalism, abbreviations are as *de rigeur* as the use of French phrases. Almost every newspaper has a *volte-face*, such as the *Natty Times*, the *Bully*, the *Fin Review*, the *'tiser*, the *SMH*, the *Sun-Pic* and the *Old Age*. You write pars for them, just as you write eps for television series. Those who would write paragraphs for television and episodes for a newspaper are not *comme il faut* in the freemasonry of abbreviations.

The ABC has its own language, as I learned when, one day over at Aunty, I called in at TV Ent only to find that the ident I wanted to see was out on a doco. It's a different world in commercial television, where an atmosphere of hype and spruik prevails. Many of the staff there are engaged in making teasers, ads and promos for their soaps and sitcoms. They read the trades and hope that p.r. will make them m.g. or media-genic.

To be *an fait* with the semiotics of modern communication you will need to do more than read a non-f. PB like this one. But if you do, it is at least a start.

4   A Tinnie Ear For Dialogue

Some playwrights are supposed to have a good ear for dialogue, particularly for colloquialisms, whereas others, those who can't slice the junket, are said to have a tin ear. Most of the adjudicators in these cases, critics and managements who assess a writer's work, are like diplomatists — they only see real people through the window of a limousine. Nevertheless, if your play doesn't sound right then you are gone. It's no use complaining that your dialogue has been drawn from life; it has to sound right and opinions on this can vary wildly. Those who would become playwrights learn early on that it's an old dog for a hard road.

The peak of Australian colloquialism is said to be 'let's crack a tinnie', meaning 'let's have a can of beer'. I have never heard the expression tinnie used seriously in real life. I asked several friends of mine, one of whom is a Queenslander, if they had ever heard the term. Like me, they had only heard it in unfunny amateur satire or used in public with conscious, scornful irony. Yet 'let's crack a tinnie' is supposed to be quintessential Australian slang because it sounds right.

Arriving at the Grafton Tennis Club early one June morning in 1985, I overheard, with my somewhat metallic ear, the following dialogue:

'Ge go out last night?'

'Air. Went down the Ex-Services Club.'

'Have a good time?'

'Oh, yeah. It was a top night.'

If I had read that dialogue I would have said that it must have been uttered by two men over thirty. Firstly, going down somewhere is exclusively male, unlike going down to or, indeed, going down on. Males over thirty in the big cities go down the pub or down the beach. Women tend to be more sensitive to the appearance of a preposition. Secondly, describing something as top is, in my experience, exclusively male and becoming slightly old-fashioned and therefore more likely to be used by an older man, expecially describing a sporting event. For example, 'It was a top game'. In a country town like Grafton, however, I discovered that theories were inadequate. The dialogue in question was uttered by two girls in their twenties. Even though I heard it live, even though the characters were indisputably real, there's still something about them that doesn't sound right. In most plays, even those written by authors who don't have a tinnie ear, language like this would be spoken by two men over thirty. It would also be applauded for its realism.

Footnote: Despite howls of protest, I hold to the view that tinnie is not the real McCoy. And what's more, I don't think footy is, either. Or telly. When I was growing up it was footer and TV. Footy and telly, I suspect, are sixties imports from Auckland and Hull, although my aunt swears that a workman at her office building in Sydney in the fifties referred to his overalls as his overies.

5 Colloquiala

A shearer's wife told me that when a woman entered a shearing shed the first man to see her called out, 'Ducks on the pond, boys'. This was a coded signal to stop swearing and smarten up. Did all the shearers' wives know this expression? Oh, yes, she told me. I pondered on the use of colloquialisms as a secret language. In Townsville, for example, there is a large army presence. The Townies refer to the less desirable elements as AJs, short for army jerks. The euphemism is a bit pointless as all the soldiers know what AJ stands for and they will thump you just as hard for calling them an AJ as they will for coming right out and declaring them to be army jerks. As a motive for using colloquialisms, secrecy is a bit sus, although I have to say I'd rather be sporting a firebreak than going bald.

A far more convincing reason for the enduring popularity of Australian colloquiala is the fact that it is colourful and good fun. Two of my favourites, for example, both come from the country, where poetic speech helps to brighten up the place. 'It stands out like a black crow in a bucket of milk', said an emigré from the North Coast, while a friend of mine from Lightning Ridge once told me that if my brains were come I couldn't duff a flea. Should I have roused on him and given him heaps? Should I have told him he was about as much use as a sun-dial in Melbourne? No, I copped it sweet and used the expression in a play, where it usually gets a good laugh.

Another feature of Australian colloquiala is the record speed with which nicknames are acquired. Vodka and orange juice, for example, quickly became known as Agent Orange when the story about Vietnam defoliants broke. In 1983 the Prime Minister, or 'Oral Robert', found his syntax had been dubbed Hawkespeak in respect of a remarkably brief time frame. Demolishing puffery is an honourable reason for switching on this vernacular. Black Jack Gibson was at his most caustic when describing media darling Paul Vautin: 'He's got a battleship mouth and a row-boat brain'.

Among the more obvious devices used in the People's Poetry is the hyphen. A low shot in golf is a snake-raper, while a soap-dodger is, reputedly, an inhabitant of the British Isles. A pillow-biter is, apparently, a resident of North Adelaide, while a philanderer is known variously as a wick-dipper or a nookie-monster.

If you're hungry enough to eat the crutch out of a low-flying duck or so thirsty you could drink paint-stripper through a straw, then you're in good company. Those who predicted the demise of colloquiala haven't been sighted off Nobby's for donkey's years.

6 Language of the North Queenslanders

Occasionally when reading a book or article on Australia I find a reference to the supposed uniformity of the country. According to the received wisdom, Australians sound the same from Weipa to Albany and from Wye-pa to All-bany. This has not been my experience. There are vast differences, linguistically, between regions in Australia, a fact which was confirmed for me during a stay in North Queensland, or North Queens-land as they say in Tasmania.

The first thing I noticed about Townsville was that everyone swallowed their iyes, like New Zealanders only not so pronounced. Whereas in Auckland they sell f'sh 'n' ch'ps and pre-loved v'deos on every corner, in Townsville it's more a case of fission chups and new electronic equupment. One other vocal quirk makes the Townies stand out and that is of course the North Queensland ay. Down south, as they say up north, people will sometimes end sentences with an interrogatory ay, which usually invites agreement. 'Hot enough for you, ay?' is normally followed by 'Air'. With the Townies, however, the reply could just as well be something like 'No, I reckon it's bloody cold ay'. The ay is not at all an interrogative and its main function is to signify that the speaker has finished and now it's the listener's turn. Ay is used all the time in Townsville, where even the local radio station is called 4AY.

Like Victorians, Queenslanders are fond of calling Newcahstle Newcastle and of course the name Castlemaine Perkins is dear to their heart. Does this mean that these two states are less Angloid than New South Wales? I'm afraid not. Victorians show a deep devotion to their governors no matter what is revealed about them, while in ultra-royalist Queensland the premier is known by some as 'the legend who'll become a peer'. Having acknowledged that Queensland is no hotbed of republicanism, it must be said that the very pure drawl which is most popularly known as 'the real Australian accent' is heard quite a lot in Queensland. Once you get used to the iyes and the ays there's no mistaking that you're in Australia. The banana benders have also supplied some vintage expressions, such as 'Do you come from Longreach?' (=

move closer) and 'He had a death adder in his pocket' (= he didn't spend much money). They call a spade a bloody shovel and a suitcase in a hurricane is a port in a storm.

Two other aspects of North Queensland language made an impression on me. One was the different meaning given to some words. For example, 'Here's a nice ripe one'll do you for tonight' means 'I'm about to sell you a piece of rotten fruit'. I was also intrigued by some of the thinking behind their use of language. A sign I noticed in a newsagency urged customers to check their change on the spot. 'No discussion will be entered into after you have left the shop,' it said, in a most ominous warning to the megaphone industry. Perhaps it's just as well we have regional differences in Australia.

In Society

7   The End of The New Class

*T*he 1970s saw the rise of a mighty empire which sought to impose its way of life on the world. But, in the way of such things, the dream of imperialism has turned to dust. The 1980s have seen the demise of this once-proud civilisation and the slow-motion drowning of its all-encompassing hopes. It was all so sudden, if we take the long view of history.

Recently, one day in the frivolous, brittle 1980s, I walked into the musty 'situation room' or nerve-centre of the old empire. It was the video studio at the Town Hall in Paddington, the Sydney suburb that seemed to have all the answers in those far-off seventies. On the shelves I found some ancient videotapes dating back as far as the winter of '74. I blew the dust off them and then there, in the afternoon light, I read the barely legible titles . . . Consciousness-raising, Kids' Workshops, Report to the Collective, Funding Seminar; and so on. Nearly all the major tribes seemed to be represented — the Iconoclasts, the Activists, the Empathisers and the Co-ordinators. The New Class empire was indeed a mighty one in its day and it was unique in that, of all the imperial forces in history, the New Class was the only one whose principal weapon was language.

What happened to these people in the eighties? What record do we have of them? Are there any traces in our current usage of some of their key words like supportive, infrastructure, charismatic, input, identity, elitist, achiever or ethnic, and what about their tell-tale compounds, such as worst-case scenario, hidden agenda, top-notch eatery, massive backlog, county-hardened, street-wise loner, troubled flagship or haunting triptych? Sad to say, very little evidence remains. Occasionally you might catch a glimpse of someone in a rusty moke selling drugs to teenagers or you may be introduced to a funding co-ordinator who's sharing a flat with a divorced female law student from South Australia. But by and large these are rare events. I was filled with emotion as I placed the faded, musty videotape back on the shelf at the Paddington Town Hall. The Age of the Aware People was over. I fear that we shall not see their like again.

8   Meet the Old Class

After the demise of the New Class the Old Class, as is the nature of such cyclical and tidal things, came back into its own. The New Class had so thoroughly blown it for the intelligentsia that many keen judges wondered if we would ever again see quality films, practise the art of dissent, or meet people who used words with more than one syllable. Here follow some aspects of the Tomato Sauce Risorgimento.

Return of the Native

After years of disgrace machismo finally came back into favour. A resurgent macho proletariat took over where it really matters — on the roads, where the cabbies, truckies, vannies and towies ruled over all the lanes. There was nothing left-wing about this coup, as two minutes' conversation with one of these Kongs of the Road will establish. Their philosophy would have precluded them from joining the Hitler Youth on the grounds that they are too immature and too reactionary.

Linguistically, Rex Mossop captured the unabashed macho spirit of the age when he declared that VFL songbird Mark Jackson would not last five minutes in rugby league: 'He's not tough enough to knock a sick girl off a chair'.

The Five O'Clock Shove

In the old days (e.g. *circa* 1967) if you got the sack you simply went out and chose another job. Not any more. The modern worker, ever fearful of 'the five o'clock shove', is more conservative. The phrase 'my job' took on more earnest intonations than in 1967, when I had about eight on the trot.

'Who do your students like best among contemporary playwrights?' I asked a drama lecturer. 'Ayckbourn,' he revealed. 'Ayckbourn??' I yelped. 'Why do they like him?' The answer was predictably stark: 'Because he's successful.'

The Carlton Diaspora

Once a hotbed [*sic*] of New Class activity, Carlton now is full of men in suits and prosperous restaurants. The Pram Factory has gone. The Australian Performing Group is no more. Most of its angstars have moved to Sydney or returned to law, medicine or teaching. In 1986 Jack Hibberd announced he was giving up the theatre to study allergies.

Walking around the streets I can still hear the old voices of the revolution. Everything else is curiously quiet. I remembered what one stalwart said of his married life with another stalwart, a union that seemed ideologically idyllic as they ruled over Carlton like a royal family: 'Brian de Palma's taken out an option on my first marriage'.

The Wandering Apostrophe

In recent years the Old Class have started to put up their own signs. No longer intimidated by the sophistication and high prices of professional sign-writers, the Old Class have decided to give it a go. A garage in East Sydney offers to fix Diff's. A store near Central sells Disposal's.

I learned about the apostrophe in fifth class at Ben Venue Public School, Armidale. But not everyone did. When we were asked to write an essay on cattle the boy sitting next to me headed his Cow's. Years later in Armidale I noticed a hand-painted sign announcing Sukeni's. Was it yet another new Japanese night-club? No, it was a vegetable market specialising in small cucumbers. Where *did* our education go wrong?

Token Pockets

Although the New Class is finished, there are still pockets of resistance to change, such as the tiny Sydney peninsula Elizabeth Bay. This is a Mecca for organised crime and gaydom, full of shoulder holsters and moustaches, where people are still interested in the doings of transsexual prostitutes. They go to the cinema, they sell drugs, they drink wine at lunch, and they believe in promiscuity. The whole place is like a time capsule. Sir John Kerr is a resident.

My friend Julie, a single Alison nearing forty, is fed up with men. 'They're all thugs or fags', she fulminated. Where does Julie live? Elizabeth Bay, of course. Julie reminds me of Jack 'Horrible' Horrigan, the old-time Rugby league player. During a Kangaroo tour of England, someone came up to him and said, 'Well, Horrible, what do you think of the Old Dart?' 'Oh, it's not a bad place', came the reply, 'but cripes, aren't there a lot of pommies around?'

The Big Renege

Not all New Class people reneged on their lifestyles and joined the Old Class. Ken Kesey maintains that drugs are highly wonderful. Papa Giuseppe still retails quiche. But the tide in the other direction is very powerful. Marsha Rowe had a baby; Yoko Ono now says that she and John Lennon were wrong to advise young people to take drugs; the *Sydney Morning Herald* actually ran a column that questioned state support for single mothers. The Big Renege was definitely on. What a pity that pillar of the Old Class, Dwight D. Eisenhower, died in 1969 when Kesey and Ono were at their peak.

Old Class Filipinas

A phenomenon of the seventies and eighties was the increasing number of Old Class males who married girls from the Philippines. Confronted with a feminist Alison or a Karen brandishing a *Cleo* and demanding multiple orgasms, some Old Class males hit on the ingenious scheme of importing an acquiescent Lily or Mae from Manila. They knew they'd get a bad press and they got it, especially in articles written by spinsters approaching forty (who called the enchanted isles The Philipenis). But the Old Class are used to getting a bad press. They shrugged it off and set about producing offspring, as the Old Class has done for some thousands of years.

The Old Left

The Communist Party of Australia has been racked by splits and defections since 1956. Two other socialist parties have broken away from it. Membership was declining. What did they do? In 1985 they bought a bloc of tickets to the Sleaze Ball and offered them at a discount to students, pensioners and the unemployed. The poor old Commos. I nearly cried. One of the sorriest spectacles is that of the Old Class trying to act New Class, especially ten years too late. What should they do? The answer is obvious. Forget all about the Sleaze Ball and merge with the Communist Party of the Philippines.

Harpy in the South

Comic Wendy Harmer came smack up against the resurgent Old Class when she performed at the 1986 Adelaide Festival. While any form of comedy is going to be in trouble in South Australia, no one could have been prepared for this onslaught by a local critic, with its peculiar use of old expressions apparently making a comeback: 'An obscene Harpy . . . a female Idi Amin — hateful, ball-tearing and sick unto death'.

Safe Quack

Two elderly female cousins of mine and a great aunt lived deep in the Sherry Belt at Potts Point, Sydney. Their idols were not film stars or world political figures but doctors. They discussed the doings of doctors as others would talk about sports celebrities. To have a specialist at a cocktail party was a coup beyond measure. Negotiating the Sherry Belt was a health hazard that faced and tested many a medicine man. One bonus, though, was that no one called them quack. Of all the Old Class masculine terms in the book, quack is the most liberating. Many Old Class males call even the best doctors 'the quack' as an assertion of liberty, equality and fraternity.

Kernel Blimp

At the centre of the Old Class revival was the increasingly aggressive marketing of junk entertainment, food and drink, especially beer. In the sixties about the only beer promotion was a languid television ad which showed some listless types around a swimming pool. The torpor was broken by a voice-over suggesting that if you had nothing better to do then perhaps a sip of Toohey's Flag Ale may be in order. This (lack of) technique has long since been superseded by the turn-your-throat-into-a-storm-water-channel ideology. When the Swan Premium zeppelin appeared in the winter skies it was a triumph. No one got out an air rifle or threw an empty bottle of cabernet at it. People just looked up at the flagship in silence. From the shivering, diseased prostitutes in the street to the mortgagees with children at private schools, from the drug lords to the husbands changing their own oil, they looked up at the symbol of schlock and they were silent.

Double Vision

If the Old Class were ever intimidated by culture, then that period is fading fast. Newcastle television heavy Lee Maughan led the way with his description of Picasso's Weeping Woman. 'It looks like a footballer after a head-high tackle,' declared the man of the people.

Vanilla Macho

Although the Old Class male dominates in the street and in the air, one thing you can bet your last peso on is that the real boss in an Old Class household is someone called Lily, Mae, Karen or Beryl.

9 Duel of the Decade: Alisons v. Karens

Division

Do we live in a deeply divided society? Is it a case of Rich v. Poor, Old Class v. New Class, Public Sector v. Private, Queensland v. The Rest? It certainly looks that way when you're having a pineapple daiquiri in the Caltex box at the State of Origin game. But what of women? Aren't they united in a powerful sisterhood? And haven't they forbidden any satire on the subject? Well, it could be that they're just like everybody else.

Image

According to the pundits the housewife with a nasal quack, a slit skirt and a name like Karen (or Debbie or Tracey or Renee) is a thing of the past. Women are wearing suits, answering to 'Alison', following careers and speaking in rounded tones about science and economics.

Reality

These pundits are either wrong or they have never had their hair cut at the Stallion Stables. The girls at the Stables, like most of the female population, chew gum, read the *Women's Weekly*, land themselves a man and retire to suburbia. The pundits, I fear, are Living in the Seventies.

Goys

Karens are mainly interested in guys, or, as they pronounce it, 'goys'. They hardly ever say 'bloke'; it sounds older and too masculine and a little bit un-American. If you're going to say 'bloke' you might as well wear a gabardine overcoat. In fact, as C.J. Dennis might have said:

Blokes and chaps, fellers and coots
Man and cove and boy
Don't bother to raise your hats
'Cause Karen only wants a goy.

No-Nos

When literary men gather they quite often talk about Karens. When Karens gather they never talk about literary men. Karens do not like men who:

wear glasses in public
pronounce the 'g' in doing
belong to a library
pat cats
pronounce two 'g's in going
subscribe to the *Spectator*
subscribe to a listener-supported FM radio station
play the piano
have seen *Rachel Rachel* twice
wear Diadora track suits
speak another language
have a name like, say, Sir Marcus Oliphant
wince when they say 'gunna'
have never been involved with organised crime

Karens say they really do appreciate men who express emotion and don't eat steak only; however, in practice, they only appreciate men who express emotion about eating steak.

Definite Turn-offs

Karens will have no truck with goys in these categories:

artists
scientists
head waiters
philosophers
ex-governors
Sir Marcus Oliphant

Borderline Cases

When Karens near thirty they'll lower their sights to include:
tattooed New Zealanders
English public school men
prisoners they're not pregnant to

Yes Yes Yes

Anyone called Kenny. For example:
Grant Kenny
Brett Kenny
Kenny Irvine
Kenny Wessels
Kepler Kenny
Kimberley John Hughes

Worldview

Karens wear slit dresses and have eyes in the back of their heads.
If I glance idly at the back view of a slitted Karen 200 metres
away across three lanes of traffic she will suddenly whip around
and glare at me.

Interests

According to feminists, the woman who was more interested in
sex scandals than science is a figure from the past. Women today
just can't get enough science, they say. Well, of course, feminists

are always right, but I have noticed one or two Karens looking just a teensy-weensy bit glassy-eyed when the subject of science comes up. Morning radio man Alan Jones reflected the spirit of frankness that is about in the eighties. He said of his audience, 'You'd have to be a snob not to admit that they're interested in gossip'.

Shotguns

These are needed to get some of the more reluctant Kennies to the altar.

They are also needed to persuade department store Karens to serve elderly bald men.

Male Honesty

Many Karens are appalled by the growing number of honest males. They aren't against honesty on moral grounds; they just worry that an honest male is not going to make it.

Besides, there's something sexless about an honest male.

Psychologists are at a loss to explain the increase in male honesty.

Karens think it's a shame. It also means they have to primp and preen to attract the few available dishonest males.

Alisons

Alisons are the antithesis of Karens. One Alison I know is very different from other Alisons. She did not seek out the one man sure to destroy her. She did not marry a gay or an alcoholic. She refused to have an illegitimate baby in a developing country. She went to a private school, sure, but she has never tried to kill herself. She has never been to a psychiatrist or married a divorced one. She had a good job, then got married and has some beautiful children. Her name is not Alison, Angela, Philippa or Gillian. Well done, Jane!

Alisons and London

London is the big question for Alisons. In fact, London seems to have been put on earth just to be a big question in the lives of Australian Alisons. To hear them tell it, London was an endless feast of art galleries and concerts. If you suggest, however gently, that the people running all these wonderful things are just a bunch of scrabblers making a living, you risk being withered in a second by an irate Alison. If only they had stayed in London — that's the Alison's Lament.

Barren Karens

Childless Karens are rare; that fate nearly always befalls Alisons. Few Karens are childless at thirty, it being *de rigeur* to have had at least two anklebiters by then (having an only child is exclusively the province of Alisons). It is a rare Karen who is unmarried at thirty; like the Royal Canadian Mounted Police, they always 'get their man'.

If a Karen remains unclaimed past thirty, she turns into an Alison and her 'job' becomes a 'career'. Her accent goes up a notch or two and the slits in her dresses start to close up. By the age of thirty-five, the gulf between her and an unreconstructed Karen becomes immense. At forty, this Home-Made Alison subscribes to the *Wine and Spirit Guide*. She has become very successful, combining the animal cunning of her Karen roots with the sophistication of an Alison.

Encounters with Karens

Len Evans tells the story of a fellow English gourmet staying at an Australian country hotel. After a heavy night he is woken at six by a maid bearing a rattling cup of tea. She asks him if he wants sugar in his tea. The English gourmet can still work up a shudder of refusal.

'Well, youse had better not stir it, then,' declared the Karen.

A friend of mine was walking through King's Cross eating an apple.

'Want a go, love?' he was asked by a prostitute.

'No thanks, love,' he said.

'You can bring your apple,' said the professional Karen.

Body Geography

Karens know whereabouts precisely their trump card is located.

Alisons don't always know what's trumps.

Karens lick their fingers when they read. They use their mouth to take off gloves and hold tickets.

Alisons use their mouth much more sparingly. And they turn pages with dry hands.

Occupations

Karens tend to work on the check-out counter at Coles New World supermarkets.

Alisons tend to be divorced from someone in the travel industry.

Language Differences

What it boils down to is this: Alisons say 'theatre' while Karens say 'live show'.

Quick Quiz

1. A top public servant on $90,000 a year is a confirmed bachelor. Then at the age of thirty-nine he actually marries. Does he marry (a) an Alison, (b) a Karen, (c) a Kenny, (d) his superannuation?

2. A tennis star on $90,000 a week marries a Karen who signs an agreement relinquishing all claims to alimony in the event of an estrangement. The Karen hears he is playing up while she stays

home with the baby. Does she (a) divorce, (b) ignore it, (c) read
the Riot Act, (d) have another baby?
(Just in case you *do* need to check, the 'correct' answers are on
page 147 in 'Notes on Contributions'.)

10 The Big Whinge

The Yukky Country

'I reckon any bloke who complains to the Anti-Discrimination
Board is a big girl', said a (semi) fictional character in an
improvised play. In Australia we have experienced peace and
prosperity since 1945 in a country with high daily average
sunshine and low incidence of Muzak. Does this make for
happiness? Apparently not. The air is filled with the sound of
whinging, everywhere from the canefields of North Queensland
to the hospitals of Melbourne. To the bemusement of the Third
World, the wide brown land shows no sign of contentment. The
psychic epidemic of whinging has taken its grip and its toll.

Scherzo for Ethnics

'I wish the New Zealanders would have a Dunkirk', said an
embittered Bondi veteran. 'They should send all their boats over
to Bondi Beach and evacuate their mates'. In ethnic matters,
everyone whinges about everyone else. Sometimes these com-
plaints take on a bizarre note, such as the claims by residents of a
Sydney suburb that Vietnamese immigrants cook stale goats on
their verandahs. Whinging Poms are legion and legend, but a
curious footnote to this saga lies with English women. These are
loudest in their condemnation of that old target, the Australian
male. Their criticisms run the usual gamut — the beer drinking,
sloppy dress, uncultured speech, the chauvinism on one hand and
the lack of chivalry on the other — but the odd thing is that
English women have great success in getting these reprobates to
the altar. A common sight in Australia is the husband who was a
bachelor till about thirty-three and his practical English wife.

Quango Infinitum

The number of boards, tribunals, departments, agencies, committees, councils, commissions, authorities, secretariats, services, centres and courts that have been set up to deal with — and encourage — whinging are far too numerous to mention. That's the whole trouble with them.

'One in Five'

This is the classic whinger's statistic, along with '40 per cent' and '3.7 per 100'. If a special interest group is set up by people with three ears then they will invariably ask for 'funding' because 'one in five' people have three ears. New South Wales Minister for Education Rod Cavalier tried to hit back at the one-in-fivers. Speaking at the annual conference of the NSW Council for Intellectual Disability, he said, 'Public Fraud Number One in the whole area of public policy in any portfolio at state or commonwealth level has been the liturgy of "one in five" '.

Some special-interest groups go further than 'one-in-five' when complaining about disadvantages. 'Forty per cent' is another favourite, used when the complainant knows that his cause is acknowledged as a strong social movement but also knows that he will never get away with anything over 50 per cent. To be the majority would, in any case, not make for effective whinging as the 'minority group' approach always sounds better. At the other end of the scale, '3.7 per 100' is an attempt at starkness. Everyone from the Service Station Towelling Employers Association to the Wheat Germ Operatives will claim that only 3.7 in 100 of their members are able to make a decent living out of their craft.

The Set-Up

Many 'reports', 'statements' and 'findings' prepared by whingers can be predicted without having to read the stuff. Farmers *never* have a good year. There is *always* a drought. Even after a month of downpours 'follow-up' rain is needed. The whinging cocky is seen increasingly as a traffic hazard in Canberra, where it seems that nothing will satisfy the farmers' representatives, not even the barrage of quangos that have been thrown their way, from the Fruit Fly Protection Board up.

There is *no* possibility, from now till the end of time, that *any* committee set up to review women's health services will report that everything is fine. Naturally, a New South Wales government committee on women's health has recommended that the Minister for Health appoint a permanent Women's Health Advisory Committee. It is not known yet when this grievance festival will get under way or whether it will be held in a soundproof booth.

Marital Status

'If you're a single woman you're either a dyke or you're on the prowl', a single woman complained to me. 'People think we're a couple of shirt-lifters', an aggrieved separated man told me after he had moved into another separated man's flat. Every state in sex and marriage has its standard whinge, many of which are daily conversation-openers.

Tautology Three

The rhetoric of whinging often leads to tautology and beyond. One example of triple-tripe comes from the Victorian Minister for Consumer Affairs, Peter Spyker, on the fitness business: 'Much of the trouble was due to a minority of shonky fly-by-night operators in the business for a fast buck'.

Company Complaints

It would be a mistake to regard whinging as the province of losers or battlers or the young at heart. Among the most active in the complaint sector are huge corporations which are hardly 'disadvantaged'. Most of the whinging centres on the government and its evil doings. Bankruptcy or falling profits are never caused by management inefficiency; it's always the fault of 'those shiny-arsed nongs in Canberra' or the 'red maggots' of the union movement. As for perks, well, these simply do not exist. A company director took out an ad in the *Sun* which pleaded for the right to 'Have a company vehicle as a reward for initiative, responsibility and performance and it be a legitimate business expense'.

Hoarse Trading

Whinging has become a standard form of negotiation. When Theatre Board subsidies are up for grabs, the grabbers stage an orchestrated battle of stridency. Community theatres say they are the Cinderellas; mainstream companies claim to be the poor cousins. Everyone adopts the outsider/minority group/destitute prostitute pose even though this is mathematically impossible.

Youth Quakes

Instead of asking them what they hope to achieve, almost every survey of young people turns into a bugfest as the questions are invariably along the lines of 'What worries you most?' and 'What is your greatest fear?'

Whinged Victory

Whinging has become so institutionalised that many radio stations air 'gripe sessions'. *Harper's Bazaar* has a page called Backlash. An indignation industry has sprung up and many lawyers will spend all their lives dealing with whingers. What happens when they get to heaven? Alex Hood used to sing a wonderful song about a whinger in that haloed place ('Look at the harp they give a man — the paint's all peeling off') but perhaps we need new myths for a new era. A modern heaven would surely be a place where one in five saints is dyslectic, 40 per cent of the angels are in need of follow-up harp-tuning development subsidies, and only 3.7 in 100 pearly-gate-servicing proprietors are currently in full-time employment.

Great Names in Whinging History

Edith Cavell protested about nurses' conditions long before Medicare.

Don Chipp said being sacked from the Fraser ministry was 'like a kick in the guts'.

Annie Cornbleet interrupted the Clissold Park School hymn and complained that its lyrics were sexist.

Ross Karp was upset about police surveillance during his biggest drug haul.

Angela Wales protested about reductions in film tax concessions.

Jim Waley produced a documentary on child abuse.

Debra Winger hated her job in *An Officer and a Gentleman*.

Digby Wolfe accused tennis commentators of lacking gallantry.

Art and Ent

*I*n tacky weeks the only entertainment to be got from television is reading the TV guides. These remarkable publications are the repository of all that is noble in our culture. Whatever else a work of art may have done in its lifetime the TV guide is its final resting-place.

Consider *Hedda Gabler*. How many students have wrestled with a précis of this classic and been daunted by its history? Not so one television guide. Here is how they described the play: 'A strong-willed woman is bored by her new husband, so she takes an opportunity to revenge herself on an old lover who is a reformed alcoholic author'.

At least they got the title and the author right. Sean O'Casey would have loved to have seen a late-night offering in one guide entitled *June and the Pastrycook*. Rodgers and Hammerstein would have been so thrilled to read they had written *My Fair Lady* they would, I am sure, have turned over the royalties from *The King and I* to Lerner and Loew.

Occasionally one gets the impression that the people who compile these guides don't know a great deal about that of which they speak. But this is only a fleeting impression, and probably a delusion. Anyway, gremlins are everywhere, causing misprints and general mayhem. Nevertheless, some people snigger when they read about *The Swiss Family Robertson* or *Birkenhead Revisited*. During Bamber Gascoigne's Christianity series one episode had Biggles overtones when it was described thus: 'Missions Abroad. With Bomber Gascoigne'.

Roald Dahl would have been surprised to find he'd directed *Chitty Chitty Bang Bang* but relieved that was the only misprint involved. Wendy Hughes once played a cerbic character and it wasn't even on SBS. What next? Probably Irma la Douche or, as an Indonesian newspaper advertised, *Gone With the Wine*.

It is easy to be critical of the various and proliferating TV guides and magazines whose compilers are, after all, just trying to do their job. And what a job it is! As Sean Connery said in an interview in the *Guardian* 'I hat incompetents'. Who can tell where they'll strike? Perhaps even in a respectable TV calumn.

They do things a little differently in the country. I was intrigued to read that a regional station was offering *Brother Sun Sister Moon*, a film about Francis of Aussisi. Presumably this new intelligence outfit will go the same way as Asio or Asis. Let's hope it won't be as anti-semitic as this description of *The Benny Goodman Story* in the same paper: 'The story focusses on Benny Goodman's rise from the Jewish area of Chicago'.

The psychological complexities of John Hopkins's *This Story of Yours* (retitled *The Offence* in the film version) were not too overwhelming for one country guide. In fact, they revelled in evey Freudian undertone: 'A cop who kills a child molester during an interrogation as the criminal had forced the detective to face himself'.

The same guide refused to tread carefully when it advertised TV Censored Bloopers. On this programme of 'flubs and goofs', it announced, the guest star would be 'actress Lyn Redgrace'.

There are some constant performers in TV guides. Actress Sondra Locke didn't change her surname when she took up with Clint Eastwood. But the TV guides change her to Sandra every time. Anyone else with a name slightly off centre can expect the same treatment, as Leo Glenn, Alex Guiness and Linda Ronson will testify, along with Alice McCowen.

Janis Balodis is a talented playwright who has not been lionised by the media 365 days a year. He's kept working well, though, and sold one of his plays to television. I was surprised to read a eulogy of it in the TV guide — surprised, that is, until I read a respectful reference to 'Miss' Balodis. Stanley Baker underwent a similar sex change operation and emerged as Stanley Baxter when he appeared in *Robinson Crusoe*. God knows how this affected Man Friday.

Neale Fraser must have been disconcerted to read in one guide that the 1983 Davis Cup semi-final between Australia and

France was to be played in 'White City, US' — no doubt a leading metropolis of the Bible Belt with a Rhodesian expatriate as mayor.

A young friend of mine from Adelaide, Suellen Pratt, is an investigative journalist who has uncovered some fascinating material about TV guides. 'Australian guides are far more gutsy and relevant than their counterparts OS,' says Suellen assertively. According to my protégé, American guides merely copy out bland film blurbs from Stephen Scheuer's book, *Movies on TV*. But not so Australian guides. There is a vast difference between these descriptions of *The Sweet Smell of Success*, the Scheuer first, and then an Australian TV guide:

Biting, no-holds-barred look at the ruthless world of a powerful and evil New York columnist. Lancaster is miscast as the columnist. This is the film in which Tony Curtis emerged as a first-rate actor and stopped being considered just another handsome Hollywood face. His slick opportunistic press agent characterisation is the backbone of this powerful drama. A much underrated film at the time of its initial release.

An underrated film at its release, it shows with verve and bite the world of a ruthless and powerful columnist. Burt Lancaster is somewhat miscast as the columnist but Tony Curtis emerges as a fine actor and not just a pretty face. He plays a slick, opportunistic press agent who's enlisted by Lancaster to break up his sister's romance with a musician. His performance gives spine to the film.

I confessed to Suellen that I could discern no great difference between the two descriptions. In fact, I said, it's almost as if Scheuer had plagiarised an Australian TV guide. But my young protégé would have none of it.

'The local version is more confrontative', she argued. 'For starters, there's an attack on the mass media in its first sentence ("an underrated film"), whereas the Scheuer version only puts up token resistance at the end.'

My assertive young friend was not finished. 'The local version attacks sexism and elitism', she said, 'viz the use of "pretty face" versus "handsome face" and "fine actor" *vis-à-vis* "first-rate actor". As well as that, "spine" is a much more gutsy term than "backbone", don't you agree?' I had to agree.

Having conceded this point I in turn had a poser for Suellen. 'Why is it', I asked, 'that Lauren Bacall is always given a good trot in the TV guides while Julie Andrews is execrated? After all, Julie Andrews is a talented actress and always superbly professional, whereas Lauren Bacall has an amateur technique and an appalling mumble'.

I pointed out to my young friend that *The Sound of Music* is referred to in many guides as *The Sound of Mucus* (on purpose) and viewers urged to turn it off for fear of drowning in an unlikely mixture of schmaltz and saccharine. Yet any number of amateurish Bacall efforts are showered with stars and given the cancel-all-engagements treatment.

Suellen was stumped. 'The only reason I can think of is that the TV guides may not be infallible in their judgements.'

I assured her that this could not be the case and then we settled down to watch *The Big Sheep*.

12 Rockley Herbert Writes for You

*T*he distinguished Melbourne theatre critic Mr Rockley Herbert was furious not to have been appointed television reviewer for the *Sydney Morning Herald*. He had been waiting for decades for the big chance to get into the box and away from the mass-produced trivia of the theatre. He had also been longing to drop a bit of Melbourne ballast into the frivolous catamarans of Sydney life.

As he told me of his thwarted ambitions tears slipped from his mournful eyes and dropped on to his 1948 gabardine overcoat. I took pity on him and offered him the post of guest critic in this book. He was touchingly grateful and after reading his piece so am I. I hope you will enjoy the insights and swashbuckling with of this truly remarkable scribe. I give you Mr Rockley Herbert:

Happy Days is a new series set in Sydney and typically superficial it is, too. I was not persuaded by the antics of Mr Henry Winkler as Bonzer, a townee with the kind of nasal twang that could only be described as Woolloomooloo Yankee. The series purports to be set in the 1970s but we are constantly distracted by the glaring anachronism of Mr Winkler's 1980s hairstyle.

Not recommended.

My colleague Suellen Pratt tells me that concerned children in Adelaide have forbidden their parents to watch *The Brady Bunch*. I can understand why. The series is superficial, tedious and dogmatic. Obviously made in Sydney, *The Brady Bunch* fails to deal with such vital issues as the Hungarian Economic Miracle.

The concerned children of Adelaide have a new ally.

Me.

One new series I have no hesitation in recommending unreservedly with no qualification whatsoever is *The World at War* on ABC TV. Here there is much to treasure. For me, the chief delight lies in Lord Olivier's virtuoso performance as 'The Narrator'. Here is a voice! At once trilling and sepulchral, the soaring cadenzas of the magnificent Olivier organ ululate scintillatingly on a chosen monotone. It is a postwar landmark.

As for the rest of the series, the weak link is the script, a not uncommon complaint. Lord Olivier is forced to use his mighty depth and breadth to airlift the narrative into the realm of global significance. In this he is successful.

See it.

The newsreader on Channel Seven is Miss Karina Kelly. This is not in itself noteworthy, nor indeed should the fact that Miss Kelly is a woman distract us from news events of global significance, such as the Hungarian Economic Miracle. Nevertheless, the fact is that Miss Kelly is a woman and as such deserves all our admiration and respect. She has mine.

Recommended.

There has been some talk that Mr Robert Baddeley Simpson has blossomed into the doyen of cricket commentators, peeling off witty anecdotes and penetrating analysis in equal measure. I do not share this view. I find Mr Simpson's analysis jejune.

Chillingly jejune.

The chairman of the ABC, Mr Geoffrey Whitehead, has been appearing as Sherlock Holmes on a commercial channel.

While it is eminently desirable that management should gain experience on the shop floor, I wonder if Mr Whitehead has not overdone things. His performance as Conan Doyle's wry sleuth is jejune in the extreme. If the ABC would care to take some advice from what it likes to call 'the capitalist press', then the advice is this:

Read a good book, Mr Whitehead.

The ABC claims it will launch a new and truly national news service this year despite the problems of staggering time zones. That is not the only problem. 76.4 per cent of the personnel chosen for this crusade are from New South Wales. You can bet these shallow galahs will concentrate on the Coathanger Capital and little else.

I only wish I could be more positive.

ATN7 is to be congratulated for screening the classic *April Love*. This is ideal summertime fare, the kind of fare at which Mr Pat Boone and Miss Shirley Jones excel. I was captivated by Miss Jones's gamine soubrette, at once *grande dame* and *belle coquette*. Mr Boone was not to be outdone and I commend his performance.

He croons, he moons, he shucks, he ducks.

Mr Henry Levin's production is admirably restrained, buoyant yet sober, evenly paced but not without its moments of relief, funny and touching yet sad and witty and erotic all the same.

Strongly recommended fare.

One of the more persuasive of our television personalities is my good friend Mr John Hanrahan, who recently screened *On an Island With You* on ATN7's *Midday Movie*. Here there was much to treasure. Two brace of *tour de force* performances from Miss Esther Williams, Mr Ricardo Montalban, Miss Cyd Charisse and Mr Peter Lawford; any amount of synchronised swimming; and a plot that was prosecuted with rigorous realism.

I understand that some members of Sydney's *soi-disant* smart set have been taping extracts from Miss Williams's output and replaying them for the amusement of their cronies. I do not like this trend. I would adjure my good friend Mr Hanrahan to speak out against this cult and shame the merrymakers into silence. I would also adjure him to present more of the Williams *oeuvre*.

Tape them with pride.

According to some so-called pseudo-intellectuals and would-be pundits, one-day cricket as televised by Channel Nine has become the Elizabethan theatre of our age.

This theory posits the Hillites as the groundlings, the Members as the court of King James, and the players as players, who, caparisoned as Harlequins, prance about for the entertainment of the multitude. Alan Border is supposed to play a character representing the aspirations of the average Sydney clerk, while Vivian Richards personifies the aspirations of the average Sydney typist. I do not subscribe to this view.

Not suggested.

ABC TV is presenting a comedy series called *Mother and Son* which has been hailed as a breakthrough. I do not share this enthusiasm. I shall refrain from dancing in the street.

And for why?

Although boasting excellent performances from Miss Ruth Cracknell and Mr Garry Macdonald (how he must hate being endlessly associated with Done Lane!), the main fault lies in the script. Mr Geoffrey Atherden has enjoyed for some time a reputation as a 'writer's writer'. He is certainly not a viewer's writer. *Mother and Son* fails to come to grips with any of the political and social and socio-political issues it raises and is totally lacking in one essential ingredient.

Punch.

I'm blessed if I know what to make of *Romper Room* (ATN7). The enigmatic central character, known only as Miss Helena (symbolic of exile? Napoleonic grandeur?) is apparently marooned in a land of little people (is she a modern Gulliver? If so, why?) whom she attempts to pacify by a series of mind games leavened with bread and circuses.

The director, Fremantle International (Fremantle who?), has set this garish spectacle for the eye in a surreal nursery on the eve of some kind of Armageddon. The noise of the approaching armies can be heard in the background as Miss Helena tries desperately to divert her small but deadly captors.

One is trying to decide whether farce or tragedy is intended when Miss Helena picks up a hollow mirror and chants 'Romper bomper stomper doo'. To me, that sounds like childish nonsense. But what the hell does it mean?

Please explain, Mr International.

It has been said that television reviewers usually have names like Nan, Fran, Shan, Dan, Geraldine Lee or Hello Mary Lou. This is not so in my case at least. The name is Herbert.

Rockley Herbert.

13 The Young Person's Guide to the Theatre: Credits

*F*or the Young Person who would become a playwright there is muich to learn of the way of the world. There is also much to learn about the practices of the good ship Theatre and the people who flail in her. Above all, the Young Person should beware of the pitfalls that Fate and Management inadvertently or advertently leave lying around in the path of those who would tell the story of their times.

The Young Person should realise from a study of the Old Testament that there is a Time for Everything. When the Young Person has a play produced there is a procedure involving credits. First, the ads appear in the paper down the bottom of the current show. There it is. *Scream* by Anodyne Thurgate. Coming soon. Then it moves to half the ad. Opening 23 July. Scream. Then the whole ad shouts SCREAM! Opening Tonite!

The Young Person can then look forward to several weeks of passing news-stands with the sure knowledge that the magic words Anodyne Thurgate are carried within. There may be a few 'hiccups', as the New Class say. For example, Janis Balodis, the Australian playwright of Lithuanian descent, was described as 'Greek-Australian writer Janos Balaidis' by theatre critic James Wayts. I usually get 'Busso' or 'Bruzer'. But sometimes the newspapers will get it right.

Then, down the bottom of the ad, the succeeding attraction worms its way in, creeping inexorably towards the heart of the rose. If you're feeling depressed towards the end of your play's run the *Herald's* Netertainment Guide will cheer you up with a good gag. The last weekend *Makassar Reef* played at the Nimrod the 'last tree performances' were advertised. 'Looks like the Final Bough', said one wit, and golly, how we all laughed! Here was the *Herald* introducing farce into a moment of tragedy, a sin their critics come down on like a tonne of aluminium.

One issue that the Australian Writers' Guild has concerned itself with is the proper display of the playwright's name in credits and advertising. This can be a two-edged sword for the Young Person of medium ego who buys a newspaper every day and heads straight for the theatre ads.

A few years ago I had a play on in Perth that was advertised in its 'coming soon' period in the normal manner. Then instead of growing gently upwards the ad suddenly featured my name in huge print along with my photo. Perhaps if I had been a Young Person of medium ego I would have been flattered. But as I was approaching what Stewart Stern calls the Last Ascending Summer I immediately smelled a rat, even from my vantage point 3000 miles away in the eastern states.

And a rat it was. With rehearsals going badly the management asked itself 'Who can we blame?' Who better than a playwright from the highly questionable eastern states?

The Young Person who would take up the theatre would do well to beware the secret language of credits. There is a time for top billing and a time to lie low.

14 Sets for Plays I Never Wrote

The following nine settings are the pivot for torrid dramas of urban living. Unfortunately the plays that take place in them have never seen the light of day, owing to the caprice of theatre managements. By themselves, the sets comprise a comment on modern interior design and the reflection of contemporary characters on the Way We Live in the suburbs of our conglomerate cities. I could, of course, be wrong.

The houses described belong to a public-relations consultant, a carpenter, a migrant teacher, an architect, an actress, a wharf labourer, a salesman, a playwright and Kevin Lenin (Kevin is a former *Nation Review* war correspondent, now a freelance activist in communal situation scenarios).

The descriptions of the settings are influenced by the following nine playwrights: Henrik Ibsen, Sam Shepard, Terence Rattigan, Bertolt Brecht, Jack Hibberd, Tennessee Williams, Harold Pinter, Samuel Beckett and Oscar Kokoschka (Oscar was a well-known Austrian Expressionist and non-smoker of the early 1900s).

Readers with half their life to throw away can try to pick which setting belongs to whom, and match the playwright to the setting.

1 The play takes place in the autumn of 1979 in a raffish *casa*, or 'home unit', in the raffish seaside area of Sydney known as the 'Randwick Quarter'.

The living-room is on the third floor and overlooks flame-tree thronged Centennial Park and the quaint, faded old 'Racecourse'. A huge chimney on the corner beside the condemned depot that used to house the old-style petrol buses throws an oblong shadow over the creased Henry Moore Exhibition poster on the old peeling cream cement render of the walls of the unit.

The soft candlelight from the traditional Formica table casts a flickering glow on the dilapidated parquet floor and overworked Toshiba 53 in the corner. Along the back wall, monsteras curl out of upended one-metre lengths of terracotta sewerage pipe filled with peat moss and yearling refuse, clutching at the bamboo blinds rolled and tied with Polytwist in front of the half-open aluminium sliding windows through which the starry, starry night can be seen.

The mewing of a cat mingles with the strains of traditional music from a quaint old 'Avoca Street Disco'.

The evocative aromas of spaghetti, toast and tom-cat drift in on the gentle sea breeze known to local folk as the 'Southerly Buster'. Occasionally, a gust of wind delivers a flutter of poignant 'betting slips' through the French windows beside the large mounted wooden rosary that rattles like a jade curtain.

The furniture is old and borrowed — a monumentally

upholstered rattan sofa built in the 1920s to house three giants lines one wall and a bookcase/disc library (from Cervantes to Santayana) the other.

The only jarring note is provided by the presence on a sanded pre-loved coffee-table of an *art deco* compote beside a Pukeberg sugar bowl of dented smoked glass, obviously gifts from a gentleman caller.

At the rise of the curtain, Bambi Fox is lying on the sofa in a silk slip singing snatches of a picturesque Gordon Parsons blues song as she prepares a written submission. There is a knock on the door.

'The set facilitated the action.'
The *Sun*

2 The curtain rises to reveal the living room of a gloomy semi-detached house in Crow's Nest, Sydney. The walls are bare and dingy and carry an air of down-at-heel gentility, of an elegance that has 'seen better days'.

There is a window up L., through which a Hills Hoist overgrown with a choko vine can be seen standing among paspalum and broken plastic clothes pegs.

Down L. is a dead mattress. The stuffing has gently subsided on to the chill floors of chipped wood and matchsticks from a thousand 'cigarettes'.

A poster of Marilyn Monroe captioned 'Killed by Pigs' lies at an angle of 45 degrees from a genteel Brotherhood of St Laurence dresser that has 'come down in the world'.

An old unoccupied wooden picture frame rail runs around under the ceiling, filled with dust and sadness at its futile destiny.

Up R. is a doorway into a kitchen of barely perceived squalor. Beside the doorway is a record cabinet where copies of *Rolling Stone* mingle with a cracked and scratched *Astral Weeks* falling through a hole in its sleeve.

In the up R. corner a once-grand bean bag lies sagging with despair at its loss of station in life.

Down R. lies a pitiful four-square of shredded sea-grass matting — all that remains of the room that used to be in bygone days a hubbub of laughter and camaraderie and cigarette 'smoke'.

From the crumbling plaster ceiling-rose dangles an Osram Carnival yellow light bulb throwing shadows across the restl͏e s bamboo outside the stained-glass porthole-style window ͏ f another era.

'The set impeded the action.'
Daily Telegraph

3 SCENE 1: LIVING-ROOM IN PADDINGTON
  CAPTION: JUNE 1976. MATT DUFF LANDS TREND WIN-
           DOWS CONTRACT. HIS WIFE LIZ BECOMES
           LUFTHANSA EXECUTIVE. THE SWEDISH
           COMMANDER OF HUSQVARNA RECRUITS
           MATT FOR GERMAN PROMOTION CAM-
           PAIGN. MATT GETS TICKET CONCESSION
           FROM LUFTHANSA. THE GOURMET'S WIFE
           BORROWS THE CROCK-POT.

'The set, and here I must absolve the furniture, facilitated the action and made it easier.'
Sydney Morning Herald

4 The rudiments of a house – walls, chairs, tables, roof.
  Photographs of Phar Lap, Les Darcy, Nellie Melba and Raymond Burr hang down.
  Hole in ceiling. Sawdust falls through.
  Chad Morgan in Dublin record on turntable.
  Hoyts axminster on floor.
  Sunlight catches the clock.
  Silence except for the clock.
  Bottles of Royal Claude Fay scotch stand on cabinet.
  Snoring can be heard.
  Father Ignoramus Gallstone SJ enters on a house-call and trips on the third bar of *I Vespri Siciliani*.
  A walnut trickles out of his lapel.
  'The set impeded the action.'
Sunday Telegraph

5 Incredible afternoon light shines past the shadow of the huge telephone exchange through the fan-light of the house beaming

on the radiata pine walls and across the Italian ceramic tiles by
the sandstock fireplace surrounded by purple Marimekko drapes
broken up with Brett Whiteley sketches of Sulawesi and a silver
M.C. Escher calendar beside the railway clock flanked by a
Balinese gamelan sitar as Scroff Prairie rides a bike through the
doorway and sends the terrarium flying off the rattan coffee-
table before landing on the sofa made from the back seat of a
1943 Studebaker covered in Jogjakarta batik.

'Vote Liberal.'

The *Australian*

6 A large house in Gore Street, Fitzroy, Melbourne, with one door
in the back wall and two in the wall to the right.

In the middle of the room is a camphor chest; in it there are
dried human heads.

In the foreground to the left is a skeleton. Beside it is a spare
skull.

Hanging from a paper lantern in centre stage is a giant razor
blade.

A small pot of dying pennyroyal decorates the fireplace.

On the mantelpiece along the left wall there are shattered
glasses and broken passionfruits.

In the south-west wall there is a door leading to a small
cemetery.

A bay window in the nor'-by-nor'-west wall looks out on a
bluestone alleyway flanked by plastic garbage bins and empty
Aquavit bottles.

In the background a gloomy fjord, half-hidden by continual
rain, can be made out.

'The set was a visually stunning knock-out that had the
audience reeling and rocking.'

The *Entertainer*

7 A room.
  A desk.
  A window.
  Autumn.
  Evening.
  Silence.

'The set was littered with irrelevant obfuscation.'
Kevin Lenin, *National Times*

8 Black house. Black street. Billowing rolls of burlap swarm up
the stairs culminating in red hessian walls torn by violent nudes
with gashed faces.

Teak staves plummet from an ashen ceiling gripping burning
torches of purple flame.

A meat hook is plunged into the back of the huge grilled oak
front door, estapolled into opacity.

Vast wooden benches line a stark table gouged by lumps of
steak and kidney pie.

A huge scarred black kettle is licked by flames from a Simpson
gas stove.

40,000 horsemen enter stage L. through a door to the garden
where stark Mexican sunflowers arch towards a thunderous sky
of molten lead torn by fierce gales that rattle the corrugated iron
of the howling, boiling roof.

Under the ravaged burlap the sanded boards coated with
Taylor's Tyre Black creak and collapse, catapaulting the horsemen into sandstone oblivion and the downstairs garage.

A woman, tall with fiery yellow hair, moves silently down the
staircase as the moaning of the chorus reaches its crescendo.

WOMAN: Time to go to work, George.

'The set facilitated the action.'
Daily Mirror

9 The curtain rises on a house by a road. Traffic. Tubular steel
sofa. Indoor garden. Ferns. Screened by glass. White plaster
walls. Quarry-tiled kitchen. Pale Scandinavian pine. A two-foot
ashtray. Metal. A fan-shaped cane throne. A baby is heard
crying. Curtain.

'The set facilitated the action by impeding it.'
The *Age.*

Local Choler

15   Cremorne: Peninsula of Gentility

It used to be that if you got into a Sydney cab and asked to go to Cremorne the cabbie would be very surprised and suspicious. 'Eh? What? Drummoyne? Eh?' They would glare at you as if you'd said Atlantis. (Sydney cabbies belong to that school of philosophical thought which holds that a cow does not exist unless there is someone to see it.) 'Cremorne', I would insist, and if I had friends or relatives with me they would back me up. 'Cremorne', they would chant. The cabbie would be most affronted. Eventually he would look up this mythical beast in the directory and discover that it was a peninsula on the Lower North Shore. He would take us there, but with an air that suggested he was only doing this to keep his licence. Why we couldn't live somewhere straightforward, somewhere with a football team, like Balmain or Manly, he just could not understand. We probably sounded a bit posh and we left no tip, but he ought to know that those people who sound a bit posh are always the meanest. The cabbies probably couldn't wait to get out of Cremorne. It was all a bit spooky for the uninitiated, and for those who believed in the homogeneity of Australian society.

I was born in the area and, despite long stints in Brisbane and Armidale, mostly grew up there, among the hundred-year-old palms and the roads named after cricketers — Iredale Avenue, Murdoch Street, Spofforth Street and Boyle Avenue. The harbour was all around, and the foreshores were largely reserves full of white gums and flame-trees. Roberts and Streeton used to live there and they painted almost every inch of Cremorne Point. The rampant Anglophilia of the early years of this century can be seen in the names of some of the blocks of flats and private hotels — The Laurels, Ranelagh Hall, Bannerman Court, The Wycombe and the Langdale Guest House. It was very much Rattigan territory, with The Laurels, in particular, being something straight out of *Separate Tables*. One time there was a fire there and they all ran out on to the footpath, retired majors, dowagers, the whole spectrum of genteel poverty and desperation. When I was about twelve I was walking along one of the harbour paths one morning with some friends and we found an overcoat and handbag. The address inside was The Laurels so we took the gear around there and discovered from the manageress that the handbag owner's bed had not been slept in. She rang the police. By the time we got back to the harbour path they were already there, and soon after the Water Police arrived in a launch. A man with long rubber gloves reached down and gripped the Laurels woman by the shoulders. They towed her away, with the pale body staying just below the surface.

Those with a passion for demographics would rank Cremorne in the middle of the middle class. Across the harbour to the south, Vaucluse (upper class) and Zetland (working class) were the extremes. We can see in the horrible example of Adelaide what can happen if an incestuous colonial gentry get together and try to create a fantasy world. The result is, among other things, stifling to art and seems to lead to sex crimes. Luckily, in Cremorne the hierarchy never really got going. It was constantly being infiltrated and modified, which was just as well, as I have heard of very few cases of a transplanted culture flourishing. It hasn't worked in South Africa, and they seem pretty miserable in Quebec. Perhaps the only contemporary success story is Bondi, where a group of New Zealand tow-truck drivers have established a society that works pretty much along the lines they're used to. But with all the different strands being acknowledged and all the exceptions noted, you would still have to say that Cremorne was very much an Angloid matriarchy where the average age was over sixty.

The middle class has not been over-mythologised in Australia. The last words spoken by Paul Hogan in his first commercial were 'Let 'er rip, Boris'. He was addressing the conductor of a symphony orchestra, a job that could only be justified by the appointment of a European. Whereas in America the Clifton Webbs, the Jose Ferrers, the Orson Welles and the Adolphe

Menjoux were allowed to play eccentrics or villains, there are very few Australian stars who are allowed to be middle-class. Yet a large proportion of them *are* middle-class. The country has been 'gentrified' but the secret has been kept: the average Australian male is much more adept at cooking shish-kebabs than at wrestling with freshwater crocs. To be faithful to the reality of Australia today, any would-be star born Chips Rafferty would have to change his name to John W. Goffage. Needless to say, the Lower North Shore has not been up there with Gundagai and Pinchgut as the icons of a civilisation. Its voice has never been heard.

People spoke very well in Cremorne and were keen to keep it that way. My mother was always at me to drop 'gunna' from the repertoire, as well as other terms I'd picked up at North Sydney Oval. My grandmother, who came from the country, had a few idiosyncrasies. A film was a pick-chore and roast chicken was the bird, there usually being much discussion about the correct time to put the bird in the oven. 'That tap wants fixing', she would say, and in general, wants had it all over needs. Her favourite radio programmes were Jack Davey's shows, but she abominated Bob Dyer, purveyor of *Give It a Go* and other aural schlock. 'Jack Davey doesn't call people by their first names', was the evidence against Dyer, who was inclined to tip buckets of water on his guests on *Cop the Lot!* My father was much more an ABC man, and his culture heroes were Russ Tyson and Sir Adrian Boult, but in 1957 2UE started its Top Forty and that was the end of radio's golden era of the spoken word. The voices on the radio now were Woolloomooloo Yankee, and Cremorne had missed out yet again.

When Sir Laurence Hartnett came to Australia in 1934 one of his aims was to make an all-Australian car. He realised his dream with the Holden in 1948, which was an instant best-seller. Not in Cremorne, however. In Cremorne there were Wolseleys, Rovers, Vauxhalls, Morrises, Austins, Humbers and Hillmans, plus the odd Studebaker and one Oldsmobile. This alienation from the home-grown product carried over into culture, where anything Australian was disdained by the middle class, who really preferred *Salad Days* to *Summer of the Seventeenth Doll*.

The most moving three words ever written by an Australian, I believe, are 'Symphony Number One' and they were written by

Alfred Hill. While upper- and lower-class humour is very similar (the *status quo* triumphs over someone who fails to treat the *status quo* with reverence), on the Lower North Shore the satirical and imaginative dimensions of middle-class humour were evident. Some of the yarn-spinners and piss-takers you would meet around the place were wonderful. I ran into one old boy from Naremburn on the Central Coast in 1986 and picked him straight away. The dialogue went like this:

'Seen Halley's Comet?'

'Nah. I saw it the first time round, in 1910. It's overrated'.

Among the younger fry in the late fifties and early sixties the favourites were Hancock, the Goons, *Mad Magazine* and Shelly Berman. Australian comedy in that era was pitiful, the problem being that it was directed at an audience of morons. Here was one case at least where the cultural cringe was justified.

One other assumption made by the middle class is that it has 'adult' tastes whereas the hoi polloi like all the kids' stuff full of sugar. To some extent they were right. Aeroplane Jelly was eaten by everyone from nine months to ninety years. When the French Restaurant opened in Sydney in 1959 the queues stretched, as they say, round the block. If anything could mobilise the middle classes it was the promise of relief from sugar despite the fact that many of them had 'uncles in Fiji'. My family favoured the Grotta Capri, and we often went there for *Scallopini di Vitello* and Quelltaler Hock. My grandmother, who was of Irish parentage, never came to the Grotta Capri. Her idea of a good meal was roast chicken and baked potatoes followed by Aeroplane Jelly.

For the youth of Cremorne, hopelessly outnumbered by the oldies, having a good time was often a problem. Sexual opportunity was limited, mainly because the girls gave very little away on the home front. There were rumours of loose behaviour on holidays in Bundanoon or The Entrance, and, in one case, the washroom at Naremburn Intermediate High, but at home in Cremorne they'd play it very straight and you'd be lucky to score a four (upstairs outside). This caused much heartburn and even now I blanch when I recall the Case of the Recalcitrant Balletomane. One of my friends made it to the big league when he took out Marsha Rowe, who founded *Spare Rib*. I thought she was the prettiest girl I'd ever seen and if it is a rule that feminists are raucous hoydens then Marsha Rowe must be the exception. In 1959 she wore a V-neck jumper that set Shellcove Road on fire.

As well as the emerging younger generation, other free agents were diluting the spirit of Cremorne, and by the early sixties it was no longer the province of the old Angloid middle class. One boy I knew lived in a semi-detached with his steam-cleaner father and buxom half-sister. He walked into the living-room one afternoon and found a sailor with his hand up his half-sister's dress. 'What did you say to her?' I asked him. He shrugged mournfully. 'Give us a fuck or I'll tell Dad'. When my friend John Scheding and I joined the North Sydney Cricket Club in 1962 we presented ourselves to the inevitable eczema-encrusted coach holding a clipboard. This old boy was *not* a man of letters and had trouble spelling our surnames. 'What's the origin of these names?' he demanded. 'Albanian', I said. 'Swedish', John said. 'Oh Sweden's a good country', declared the coach, relieved. At one stage a rich legal family moved into our street but this invasion ended in a very Cremorne-ish way. The father was electrocuted when he poked a fork into a toaster and the mother moved in with a Yugoslav migrant in a house overlooking the reserve.

The biggest house in Kareela Road was owned by Mrs Chuey, a tiny, rich Chinese widow from Junee, who shared the wonderful Victorian mansion with her brother-in-law. The Chueys were good fun, holding mah jong parties and taking my aunt to Chinese New Year celebrations at the Trocadero Ballroom, but eventually the brother-in-law went to China to die and Mrs Chuey sold out. The house was then razed and a new one, all glass and tile, white carpets and roll-a-door, was occupied by a businessman and his second wife. This happened in the mid fifties and was very much a portent. By 1975 the dilution process had become a wash-out and many of the Edwardian bungalows had made way for units, town houses and so on. The area became popular with the TV push, Qantas staff, businessmen and their third wives, advertising executives and American Express pharaohs, some of whom were our good friends or tennis partners. But we had long since moved out.

My big break with Cremorne came when I started writing
plays. I announced my intention to make a living by writing plays
set in Australia — and make a bloody good living, too. This
announcement did not go down well with my family circle. The
course I was plotting for myself was unknown to the area. There
had been a few cases in the post-war years of eastern suburbs
families standing by helplessly while one of their sons or
daughters ran off to London and got involved in stage design for
Sadler's Wells, but my case — that of contemplating Australian
life and language as a subject for art — was unheard of.
Politically, Cremorne was one of the safest Liberal areas in the
country (my mother used to refer satirically to the Labor leader
as 'Old Cocky Calwell'), so my intention to write plays in the
rationalist/anti-colonialist style was definitely not simpatico. Nor
was my appearance on Doris Fitton's doorstep with a copy of my
first play. 'Ay do not receive visitors' at may prayvate residence',
said the artistic director of North Sydney's Independent Theatre.
Seventeen years later, in 1984, *Coralie Lansdowne Says No* was
successfully revived there and I have to admit I lingered a bit in
the foyer afterwards. Poor old Doris had gone and all her
European plays with her, but there was still something uncon-
quered about that foyer. Any victory over the middle class is a
temporary one, as is any exit from the Lower North Shore.

16 Townsville: Beyond Thunderbox

Among the smells of a Townsville suburb in early evening are
frying onion and damp brown grass. The pink trumpet trees look
fatigued, as well they might after another long bout with the sun.
In a few of the stilted houses they are having curry or satay and
some of the grass is green and dry, but for most householders
this time of the day is given over to watering the burnt lawn as a
prelude to steak and mash.

The sky in Townsville is all gong and no dinner. It will often fill
with pregnant grey clouds but there won't be a drop of rain. The
city is in a rain shadow and in the dry tropical air the sound of

parrot screeches from a thousand laundries travels fast. Later on the night sounds include a possum with emphysema and the piercing lament of the curlew. Presiding over all this is Castle Hill (the locals pronounce it to rhyme with Hassle Lil), a big rock masquerading as a mountain. The crags and scars are so visible, so stark, that they recall an old man who has not deigned to keep bandaged up after a skin cancer operation. Even walking along the shopping mall in the centre of the city you can feel the baleful glare of the big rock and sure enough, there it is, reflecting on a store window full of crockery specials. Behind the rock there are a few million hectares of brown plain.

Townsville (the name sounds tautological but it was discovered by Robert Towns) is in a political shadow, too, being a Labor electorate surrounded by what the commentators like to call 'National Party strongholds'. In Queensland Joh has routed the left and it comes as a surprise to find Labor in charge at all levels of government in Townsville. Queenslanders don't call him 'the Premier' or 'Sir Johannes Bjelke-Petersen' or 'the legend who'll become a peer'. It's just Joh and Flo and now son John, a rural media freak who is fond of toasting the Queen in orange juice while the cameras are running. In many parts of the world in the eighties the left has self-destructed, but not in Queensland; Joh decided not to leave anything to chance.

Despite the hostile environment the Town Mayor, Alderman Mike Reynolds, is an unruffled Dickensian figure with a substantial physique and huge mutton-chop whiskers. His verbal style is quite Dickensian, too. Speaking of an older suburb across the river, His Worship said, 'I would foreshadow that South Townsville has a most optimistic future'. The pace of North Queensland politics is Victorian, too. I rang one local pol to give him a message from a friend in Sydney. He was out, so I left my name and number with his secretary. A week passed. I rang again, and this time I cornered the pol. Did he get my message? Oh yes, but he didn't think I wanted him to ring back *that* quickly. In North Queensland a week in politics is a short time.

In contrast to, or perhaps because of, the slow pace of life the pop art of town commerce is more striking than any I have seen. Above a butcher's shop called 'Laurie's Meatland' a huge cow revolves, a sacrifice in the war against apathy. The Mansfield

Hotel has a silo-sized can of Foster's Lager on its roof, while a saddlery lurks under the shadow of a gleaming black stallion. It is almost pre-literary in effect, a leap back to the Middle Ages when tradespeople advertised their product with a drawing or a sculpture. On the roof of 'Movie House' there is a life-sized model of a cameraman with 1971 side-levers and a baseball cap operating a big black multifaceted movie camera. Americana is much admired by these pop-art spruikers; from the mural on Nevada's Steakhouse to the neon portrait of Colonel Sanders, there is overwhelming evidence that American popular culture has not been driven underground.

As if to compensate for these visual coups, there are many post-literal signs, too. A suburban tennis club has a large one over its entrance which reads 'Suburban Tennis Club'. The Wandering Apostrophe has not been domesticated in Queensland, I discovered. One of my favourite signs was on a catering caravan, the Busy Bee, which could be hired for

★ Fete's
★ Rodeo's
★ Show's

The Mall, haunted by warm sea breezes and atonal buskers, is the usual jumble of scuffed benches and jigsaw paving stained with icecream falls. The pop art here is muted and syndicated (Coles, David Jones, Stefan), although one newsagent has broken through with a hand-printed 'Notice to Customer's'. Although it is a city of 100,000 with substantial mining and tourism industries, Townsville is still a country town when it comes to putting on a bleak Sunday. I saw two American tourists picking their way through the empty Mall late on a windy, cloudy weekend. They looked like nuns in Greenland.

Unfortunately for the character of Townsville, the Mall style of architecture has taken over from the authentic Queensland gothic of stilts and wooden slats with a hundred shadows and a peeling thunderbox at the bottom of the yard. Some of them remain, as do the thirties-homage blocks of flats with rusty balconies, and it is these that give Townsville a home of its own. Otherwise you could be anywhere.

The people, too, are changing, but not as quickly. In fact, nothing is quick in North Queensland and all the go-ahead Americanism is soon revealed as a veneer. The heat and the isolation have produced a certain slowness of mind and speech, a 'mañana' mentality in the only white Protestant city in the tropics. The population is largely Angloid, and if you've ever wondered what causes poverty in warm countries, whether it's Catholicism, Latin inefficiency, Asian fatalism or inertia brought on by the heat, then Townsville can clear up the matter. It's the heat. The Protestant work ethic is viewed congenially, but stops short of being an engulfing philosophy for the majority, most of whom cannot tell you the date. Watching the children walk barefoot down the middle of the road on their way to school, and knowing that only 4 per cent of them will go to university, you realise that change from within will be slow. In the meantime, life goes on; I was introduced to a man in shorts who would organise publicity for a drama workshop I was doing, I was told. I bumped into him some days later and he eventually remembered who I was. 'Getting any publicity?' he asked in genial tones. 'Yes, actually, there's an interview with me in today's paper', I was able to tell him. He was genuinely delighted. 'Is there? Oh, I must get a copy', he resolved.

By this stage I had learned a few tricks. In Town you buy young wine and old meat, never wear a tie, carry a calendar in your wallet, stay off the Barbed Wire (Fourex beer), and don't expect the average person in the street to be anything other than a friendly non-candidate for a PhD. You also don't wear a corduroy coat to a government high school, where the students get around in shorts and micro-skirts and can't spell discipline. One night I heard a boy and a girl from Townsville High on the radio. 4TO (774 on your dial) was conducting a quiz in the Who-Am-I format and the contestants had to say '4TO' or '774' if they thought they knew. The compere started off, 'I was born in Edinburgh in 1830, etc.' and after a few more clues the boy said '774'. What was his answer? 'Robert Towns.' No, it wasn't, they were told. On they went, and the character was practically on his deathbed when the girl suddenly said '4TO'. The compere was delighted. 'What's your answer?' he asked. 'Robert Towns.'

'We'd open you with welcome arms', said an ebullient

secretary at an unlabelled suburban tennis club. Sport is the most popular activity in Town, and whatever the Townies may lack in the intellectual stakes, they make up for it in enthusiasm for their sport. Anyone from a country town knows that to get anywhere or meet anyone you have to join either a sports club or the amateur dramatic society. It is thus in Town and they throw themselves into everything from tri-athlons to indoor cricket. Tennis is well established, and is called 'fixtures ay'. I told the ebullient secretary that I'd like to play comp, and she said, 'You want to play fixtures ay?' I said that I did, 'Well then, I'll put you down for fixtures ay', she declared. I found temperaments a bit more restrained in fixtures ay than they are in Sydney. A girl on my team agreed. 'We just stamp our foot when we do our nana', she explained. Later on she asked a woman in the opposition what she had on her farm. 'Cows', was the reply, 'Cows and boongs'.

On my first day in Town I went down to a small clump of shops on the main road, where the trucks thunder in from Mount Isa, interspersed with cars from Charters Towers and bikes from some of the wonderful Town suburbs like Mysterton, Oonoonba or Belgian Gardens. They found a bottle of red wine for me in the liquor store, much to their pleasure and surprise. Children playing in the dust and sun seemed friendly enough except for one boy of about ten who is lolling about outside the liquor store. He is black, of some kind of island mixture, and already built like a rugby forward. 'Hello *brother*', he sneers, and my reflex 'Hello' seems fairly hollow under the circumstances.

Rugby League is the Aborigines' sport and Palm Island, their reserve, fields several teams. The firsts are captained by Vern Daisy, a popular character in the north playing his last season, and they make the semis, much to the delight of their supporters, who wear colours that whites would never dream of. The pale green field with its ochre running track is surrounded by a riot of pink dresses and violet shirts as Vern Daisy leads out Palm Island to do battle with WEA's (their apostrophe). Alas for Palm Island, the incontinent-sounding WEA's beat them 54-22 in one of the season's highest-scoring games. Exit Vern Daisy, rugby league legend.

On the other side of the coin, the amateur dramatic movement has all but petered out. In the fifties and sixties the popular North Queensland Drama Festival was held in Town, with groups competing from the Isa, Mackay, Cairns and Ayr. Now the touring shows — nearly all American musicals — coming into the new civic theatres have drained away a lot of the audience. One of the local directors is 'rehearsing *Streetcar*' and there is, inevitably I suppose, an Englishman in boots producing *Equus* for a local group, but few Australian plays are considered. The periodic desertion of the brittle middle-class audience is something theatre people get used to, especially in the North, and once again it has been left to Slim Dusty to carry Australian culture on his back.

The Pacific Festival is held in September and consists mainly of sporting events and attractions for the tourists from 'down south' (a phrase that is never flattering). The centrepiece is a team game based on *It's a Knockout* (as seen on TV!) and called *Almost Anything Goes*. The Sunday at the showground is not one of the better country-town Sundays. A cruel wind wrecked the day effectively, but the participants seemed to accept this as inevitable and enjoyed the laboured madcappery as much as they could. Detergent from the greasy slide blew everywhere, suds flying all over the radio gear, but the announcer boomed on, unfazed by yet another bad hand dealt by the elements. If the people of Townsville are slow and suspicious they are also great endurers. Like the big rock, they'll be there at the finish.

NOTES: WEA's stands for West End Athletic's (their apostrophe). J.M. Black, business partner of Robert Towns, was born in Edinburgh in 1830.

17 The Big Apricot

*T*he Shore Motel is set among the gums of Artarmon. The walls are a stampede of white stucco and black-ribbed coach-lamps. The roof is of Spanish tile. It was here that I went to a wedding reception. As the groom was a policeman, so were most of the guests, and the air was full of in-jokes about some notorious division and the quality of its leadership.

In the other convention rooms the pyramid game was being played, the aim of which, broadly speaking, is to climb to the top on the backs of suckers who climb after you on the backs of suckers. The Shore staff gave impartial service to all their clients.

The pyramid game was raided and as police from some less notorious division moved in, well dressed pyramid players scuttled away into the dark under the gums, past the less-than-Grecian fountain, and took their chances among the headlights on the Pacific Highway.

If you had to sum up Sydney — and the unreflective Sydneysiders never do — then this night of faltering glamour would be it. All the processes of the city — the cops and gamblers, the business ethic, the lottery they call the law, the artificial and natural settings, the rowdy good humour, the lack of malice, the sporting spirit, the dazzling front that ends in a midnight flit were served up for all to see.

Leaving aside the city's processes, I took a few days off and went looking for its sound. Okay, so there isn't one. But there are some beautiful and fascinating slivers of glass to go in its place, and the memories of some kind of life will never fade.

Sydney is great, as long as you aren't one of those people who are 'looking for something'. In Sydney, in fact, there isn't 'any thing'. You have a choice between visibility and invisibility, and that's about it.

Long Bay is aptly and preemptively named. It is so long and narrow that the waves are a discontinued line well before they reach the sand. There is hardly any show of white as they flop spent on the beach. The scrawny hills that dip low on either side are covered with clumps of wiry tundra, while at the water's edge poisoned shellfish and a few rugged, determined snails take their chances. The sewerage is clearly demarcated and the canoeists on the bay can see it like a relief map. Inland is Long Bay Jail. Over the hill is where Chips Rafferty led the charge during the 'location' filming of *Forty Thousand Horsemen*.

Following the ancient trail around to Botany Bay involves picking your way through a sprightly maze of power stations, oil refineries, dredging rigs and lowflying aircraft, with glimpses of pale blue and white on the bayside. Brighton-le-Sands is typical of Sydney's south shore. It is tougher, industry comes first, and the waterfront is sturdy, windblown and English. By comparison, the hedonistic northern beaches — Bilgola, Avalon — seem dilettanteish and uncommitted, heading for a shock awakening.

A fat man in tie and coat stumps along the beach at the Sands. In full view of a restaurant he changes laboriously into swimming trunks and wades in for a hardy winter swim. It is like watching two polar bears fighting on top of a tarpaulin. After this constitutional, he changes back into his coat and tie and trudges off, oblivious to the running commentary provided by the waiter in the restaurant.

This shameless, unconcerned, seen-it-all, show-it-all behaviour touched off a memory. I recalled the Case of the Unabashed Crone. In this adventure, the theatre director Ken Horler and I were having a few beers after rehearsal at a pub. The script of the play was on the bar and we referred to it animatedly and often. Sitting beside us was an Unabashed Crone who was eventually moved to pick up the embattled script.

'What's this?' she demanded.

'It's a play'.

'What's it called?'

'Um ... *Rooted* ...'

A flicker of thought passed across the rugged features.

'How many times?' enquired the Unabashed Crone.

Trying to escape these endless associations I booked a ticket on the good ship *Captain Cook II* for a tourist cruise of the harbour. Here at least I would see the city as newcomers did. The epic voyage did not begin auspiciously.

On the day I was there, Jetty 6 at Circular Quay was not the greatest advertisement for the Summer City. There is a half-eaten meat pie lying abandoned on its side on the cracked and stained cement floor, which is awash with fast-drying chocolate milk. Huddles of Americans and Japanese stand about waiting for something to happen.

'No credit cards. Company policy,' says the plucky pseud behind the desk.

Of course not! After all, this is the travel industry. Credit cards were designed for rare book sales, although lately milk-bars in Normanton have been accepting them. I reason with the pseud that it would be a bore to go to the bank and draw cash, but I get a replay of the company line. In no time at all we are as cosy as John McEnroe and a line judge.

Carrying a lighter wallet, I join the foreign legion under a sign which says 'Sydney Smiles'. There is a crash and a shudder and a groaning of pylons; the *Captain Cook II* has arrived like a bulldozer being driven by Zero Mostel. The good ship is not all that prepossessing; the tables are topped with Channel Steamer laminex and the carpet is early Leagues Club — as if a thousand snails have been crushed and then topdressed with lime cordial.

But soon we are out on the harbour and, as they used to say of Manly, a thousand miles from care. Even the carpet looks beautiful in this glorious setting. I try to see it through the tourists' eyes but fail. The gnarled foreshores contain at least one memory per fifty metres. My first cigarette! My last shipwreck . . .

I went back to Middle Harbour Public School in Cremorne to see if it was still the same. The main building still presides over the most magnificent view any school ever had: two tall palms and then the harbour spread out under the sunlight in sensible shades of blue and gold. As in my day, the children dash back and forth without noticing it.

I chat to the secretary and then she shows me the register, where pupils' names have been written in pen and ink since 1916. I learn from the fading parchment that I enrolled for kindergarten in May 1949 at the age of four years ten months. Always vain about my infallible memory, I tell the secretary that I sat across the aisle from a girl called Ann Carter. She checks the register, and there it is in grey and yellow: Ann Loader.

I seem to recall seeing Dean Martin and Jerry Lewis films at the Prince Edward in Castlereagh Street and then wolfing down blue icecream in the Sapphire room of the Hotel Australia opposite, but there is no sign of these places now. I must have been wrong . . .

On board the *Captain Cook II*, a middle-aged American dressed in flour white except for a slouch hat stares at the gums and balconies of Hunters Hill like a flying doctor at a christening. Along the Lane Cove River the old sandstone verandah houses have battened on to the crests of the hills while the newer, more rugged luxury houses have pushed in on the waterfront.

The hostess, a pleasant girl with a mid-Tasman accent and a well organised defence, tells us about the coal deposits under the harbour, the South Sea coal just waiting to save the economy in 1995 with, no doubt, the full approval of the environmentalists. Some of the tourists ask her questions about this, but she smiles and moves on, launching into a story about the convict Billy Blue.

The commentary rains around a thoughtful Japanese girl who blinks impassively at the cranes of Cockatoo Island. She is apparently untouched by the moving story of Birchgrove's comeback. Nor is she galvanised by the story of former convict Mary Reibey's business success. This is the old standby of the non-partisan cause, the story of a successful female capitalist. The left can't knock Women; the right can't knock Free Enterprise. The Japanese girl is apparently in the centre . . .

I remember when a friend of ours, the Carlton Girl, came up from Melbourne and we showed her around. Sydney just went in one eye and out the other. The Hawkesbury might as well have been a storm-water channel. She ate pineapple doughnuts with her oysters. This is not to say, however, that she didn't have a finely developed sense of aesthetics.

At a party for some visiting English actors, the Carlton Girl met Patrick Stewart and was most impressed. Patrick looks like Lenin and played Lenin once, but he also looks like Clement Attlee and played Clement Attlee once. The Carlton Girl could only see the Lenin side of him. He had 'depth'. Jack Thompson, another guest at the party, was 'superficial'.

Another Sydney writer and I took issue. Outnumbered, the Carlton Girl fought like a Trojan beaver on heat. 'Come on', we said, 'surely most women would find Jack Thompson more attractive'. The Carlton Girl insisted that it was the opposite with her, that Thompson was plastic, cosmetic, unreal. 'After all', she said for a clincher, 'you guys don't find those nymphets in the Coca-Cola ads attractive, do you?' 'Oh noooo,' we replied in the best Carlton manner. Satisfied she had won her point, the Carlton Girl went off to refill her glass. Later we discovered her deep in conversation with Timothy West, famous for his television portrayal of Edward VII.

As the *Captain Cook II* furrows around Rodd Island, the hostess continues her commentary. As in a Beckett play, the main character is off-stage. This is the amorphate 'they'. 'They' are restoring Darling Harbour. 'They' have decided to build a new bridge. 'They' sent Mary Reibey out for stealing a bridle. 'They' put everything in containers these days. 'They' have recycled a lot of buildings in the Rocks area. I am reminded of the Porky Pig cartoon where Porky begins a phone call 'Hello? The authorities?'

But there is something rather interesting about this commentary, which is mostly well written and well presented. At first it seems full of tales about convicts and colonial entrepreneurs. The tourists are being shown some colourful outpost of civilisations. But as it unfolds, something is missing. The Cultural Cringe. The unspoken thought is there: isn't this all rather grand? And doesn't it stand up by itself rather well?

This commentary doesn't evoke Vancouver or Auckland or Paris, for that matter. It's Sydney, take it or leave it. None of the tourists gets an opportunity to be condescending, an element I have seen in Vancouver, Auckland, and Paris, for that matter.

As we near the home stretch, even Pyrmont seems, well, busy. I catch a glimpse of the Trades Hall, and recall the adventures of another Melbourne character let loose in the Coathanger Capital.

This happened at the, wait for it, Annual General Meeting of the Australian Writers' Guild in the George Hunt Room of the Trades Hall. John Smythe, a Melbourne man who was on the APG Collective at the Pram Factory Theatre, gapes in aureal wonder as the Treasurer's Report is not fully tabled or circulated. In Melbourne, meetings are a way of life, and John has settled in for a six-hour closed session.

In no time at all the meeting is over and we are revolving around the drinks table. Smythe is stunned. He beards Tony Sattler, the car snob who wrote *Kingswood Country* (RS Productions). Sattler, self-appointed chairperson of some kind of Clothes Justification Tribunal, pauses in his condemnation of someone's Hush Puppies long enough to answer a question of Smythe's. I miss the question, but catch the answer. 'For the money', Sattler says. Smythe looks shattered, as if he's never heard this before.

What was the question? Sattler is busy criticising sports coats on the other side of the room when I finally get the answer from Gary Reilly, the R of RS. Was it anything about sex? No, the question was 'Why do you write?'

I look across at John Smythe. He is a shocked and beaten man, stumbling among Philistines who care not a whit for a finely turned motion. Then I look across at Sattler, who is rubbishing an ageing screenwriter's formerly white sweater. Why do they all come to Sydney, these Melbourne idealists like Smythe? 'For the money', I seem to hear Sattler answer, brushing fluff off a blue polyester coat that painstakingly recreates the feel of 1961.

What I sense John misses is procedure and permanence, what he gets is anarchy and plastic. He's probably used to rituals like the Melbourne Cup, that solemn orderly pursuit of money and pleasure, where everyone knows his place and eats the same thing every year, where the pyramid game is foreign and abhorrent.

Is it possible to crystallise these differences? Probably not. One of many legends about Hollywood writers concerns the wife of a prominent scenarist. On a trip to Europe she became enamoured of bidets and cabled her husband to buy one for their home. He cabled back: 'No bidets available in LA: suggest you take shower standing on hands'. Faced with a similar predicament a Melbourne man would dictate a letter to the Paris branch of Royal Doulton: a Sydney man would either steal one from the French Consulate or start chipping away at the bath, depending on whether he lived north or south of the harbour . . .

As the *Captain Cook II* pancake lands at the long-suffering Jetty 6, I ponder a few far-from-eternal questions. Why do people live in Sydney? Because the alternatives look sicker every day is the usual answer. In my case, I never really moved out. I know the place is crass. I know it's corrupt. I know you could fire a cannon down Hopetoun Avenue, Vaucluse, or Parramatta Road, Auburn, and never hit anyone who's read a book. But I love it, and I know I'll probably never leave it.

At the Shore Motel in mid-afternoon the magpies and the traffic share the noise. The place is quiet inside. The staff pile up cutlery in the convention rooms. A few diners linger over coffee in the putative Mediterranean restaurant. Children play in the pool beside the absurd fountain. Out in the courtyard, I notice the back wall is of red brick, with aluminium windows. At the Shore

Motel, no one knows anything about any pyramid game. Play is continuous, and there will be no undue interruption.

18 The Big Tomato

*B*y Rockley Herbert

For those who might not know — Eskimos, perhaps, or oil riggers on leave — I was Melbourne born and bred. As a scourge of Sydney and ongoing cynic about the prospects for the Coathanger Capital I am often asked, 'Why don't you go back to Melbourne? Why live in Sydney?' The answer is simple.

I like the pain.

When the Swans moved to Sydney I rejoiced. Here was a chance to see some real football. But any thoughts I may have entertained about a bit of good old Melbourne propriety among all the Sydney ballyhoo have been laid to rest. The Swans are owned by a millionaire with a young blonde doxy on his arm. They have made a series of television commercials in which crassness appears to be the paramount consideration. And now we have the Swanettes.

Oh well. You've got to fight fire with fire, I suppose.

It's Broadcasting Tribunal time again. Time for every crazy in the woodwork to crawl out and abuse Rupert Murdoch and his wonderful paper, the *Daily Mirror*. What do they hope to gain from these shenanigans?

Easy.

Free publicity for their loony tunes in one of Mr Murdoch's outlets.

They say familiarity breeds contempt but I have a contempt for familiarity. The other day a young lout approached me in Hyde Park as I strolled past some young secretaries sitting on the grass. 'Well Rockles,' he leered, 'Which one do you fancy?'

Spell in the navy might do these types some good.

One of the most agreeable customs in sunny Melbourne is the Levee. This is a guided 'open day' in which the more prominent of the citizens of that fair city call on the Governor. The dignitaries are able to chat to His Excellency and keep him abreast of financial and electoral affairs. You don't find anything of this sort in Sydney.

Not 'ethnic' enough, I suppose.

Australia's greatest artist is without doubt the legendary Barry Humphries. Yet some there are who would have none of this. According to this school of thought we now know that Melbourne in the forties was extremely dreary so that further bulletins from Mr Humphries are redundant.

I say this is tosh.

Melbourne in the forties was *not* extremely dreary. Here was a peak of decorum. Here there was respect and civility on a scale unknown in Tinseltown. No, the real target of Mr Humphries' expert barbs lies elsewhere.

Somewhere near Port Jackson.

The Lord Mayor of Sydney, Alderman Doug Sutherland, is an enigma. He has established his humanitarian credentials by banning dwarf-tossing and promoting that cinematic stiff *The Return of Captain Invincible*. He has given a timely reminder of our links with the old country by appointing a Town Crier, who has proved a wonderful contrast to the plethora of Lebs and Balts on the throne at the Town Hall in the seventies.

But His Worship has unaccountably failed to place a bounty on the head of Franca Arena MLC, who has suggested 'ethnic' names for some of our city streets and squares.

You can say one thing for sure about Alderman Doug Sutherland.

He is an enigma.

It has been said that my literary style owes a great deal to the Victorian chauvinism of ex-playwright Jack Hibberd and the Victorian syntax of ex-theatre critic H. G. Kippax.

This is bosh.

Sydney bosh.

Many theatrical luminaries have left Melbourne for the pearls and oysters of Sydney. Some say it's for the sun or the money while others cite the state of their liver.

Sydney playwright Alex Buzo is an exception, lobbing regularly in Melbourne for one thing or another. I suppose I should applaud Buzo for his good taste, but something stops me.

Something unspoken.

England had the Rev. David Sheppard in the sixties and now in Dean Jones we have our very own cricketing cleric. He's a Victorian boy, too. I was disconcerted to see him drop a few catches recently, a weakness he shares with the good Sheppard.

You'd think they could choose some other moment to close their eyes in prayer.

Still, if you have to play in front of a Sydney crowd you need some kind of faith.

The *Age* Tapes are dynamite. They blow the lid off New South Wales and reveal it as the Nevada of the commonwealth. Naturally they were first published in Melbourne.

What price the *Mirror* Tapes?

Fat chance.

Satirical figures are popularly supposed to have names like Wal Hughpole or Roberto M. Cohan III. I once heard of a *Time* magazine parody which was written by Talbot E. Rosenblatt, P.J. Foxglove Biltmore and Beverley Grimaldi Vandenberg. Such extravagance is not so in my case at least.

The name is Herbert.

Rockley Herbert.

19 Encounters with South Australians

Catherine Wilson of Adelaide sat next to me at a dinner to wind up a drama conference. I took the unwise step of introducing myself to her. 'I know who you are', she said, 'I went to your first session'. No others? 'No, because it was obvious you weren't going to get anywhere', she explained compassionately.

A friend of mine thought he had landed on his feet in Adelaide. Within two hours of arriving there he was sharing a shower with a sixteen-year-old girl. However, he ended his first day in the Garden City running away from a would-be rapist.

Reg Livermore was booed in Adelaide because they thought he was anti-gay.

Trudy the German theatre-restaurant proprietor from Adelaide waylaid a couple of customers and asked if they had enjoyed the evening. Very much, they said, especially the show. What about the food? They hadn't enjoyed the food so much. Trudy, who is overweight and has never seen a play worth the name, snorted and honked. 'What would you know?' she spat, 'You're only customers'.

One of the members of my cricket team has a girlfriend who comes from Adelaide. One day she actually came to a game. When her boyfriend went out to bat she called out to him *'Bonne chance!'*

Only a South Australian would wear a pink shirt with a 1960 tie-pin on *Sportsworld* and demonstrate knee surgery in living colour. 'Now go and carve the roast', advised a grimacing Rex Mossop.

Overweight journalist Tony Baker described Adelaide as 'the capital of sexual democracy'.

A South Australian woman offered herself as a 'catalyst' (her phrase) for one of Adelaide's many sterile couples. 'I'm not happy unless I'm pregnant', she said.

A NIDA student was the only holdout as people congratulated actor Peter Carmody on his performance as Norm in *Norm and Ahmed* at the first preview. Why? He thought the Norm in his local Bordertown, SA, teachers' college production was much better, the shy lad explained to the ebullient Carmody.

An Adelaide woman (called Kate) was refused service at a gay bar in Sydney. Displaying the sense of priorities that is making her state famous, she wrote in a letter to the editor of the *Sydney Morning Herald*, 'Surely this attitude benefits neither homosexuals nor the State of New South Wales'.

The Pirate Movie was disowned by its screenwriter, Trevor Farrant of Adelaide, who said the producer 'inserted phallic and homosexual jokes *which I didn't write*'.

When singer David Bowie was in Adelaide an ardent admirer rang and asked if he could see the specialist in ambiguity. The admirer ended up spending an hour in Bowie's suite. Who was this privileged fan? South Australian premier John Bannon.

Casting around for something she liked about Australia, veteran screenwriter Fay Weldon put at the top of her list 'South Australia's social legislation'.

I was intrigued to read the following in a newspaper: 'An Adelaide man convicted of theft will undergo medical and psychiatric tests to decide if his request to be sent to a women's prison should be granted'.

If you asked me what I thought was a typical South Australian man's name I would say Ashley Irwin. A typical woman's name would be Fred Quimby.

An Adelaide actress used to write newspaper articles under the pseudonym 'Ms Haversham'. She felt she had a lot in common with the spinster in *Great Expectations*. I mentioned to her that Dickens spelt it 'Miss Havisham'. Was her deviation deliberate? Yes. She said she wanted the name to suggest someone who would 'have her sham'.

At the Sixth Australian Statistical Conference Dr A.W. Davis of

Adelaide spoke immediately following afternoon tea on 'Randomisation Aspects of Nearest-neighbour Experimental Designs'.

Ashley Mallett and Ashley Woodcock both played cricket for South Australia in the 1970s.

'What a superb piece of direction', remarked a bright young Adelaide thing in overalls during the interval of a production of *The Three Sisters*. 'He's got all the women down one end of the room and all the men down the other.'

On a visit to Adelaide a friend of mine allowed his hosts to get some take-away food for him. 'We got you a quiche, John', they announced in mixed company.

An Adelaide Person brought a new dimension to four centuries of Shakespearean analysis at a recent drama conference. 'Hamlet is sexist', revealed the AP.

At a meeting of The Women And Theatre project an Adelaide 'woman' claimed that some participants had been 'sleeping with the enemy'. An actress then ran sobbing to the loo.

During a performance of a play of mine a door fell down. The stage manager, who was born in Adelaide, then spent ten noisy minutes on stage fixing it.

The male population of South Australia — never very high — declined significantly during the 1970s. Why? According to one of those who fled: 'The State Government made homosexuality legal. We got out before they made it compulsory'.

South Australian football commentator Dave Darby described vividly the impact of a series of setbacks on one team. 'They had the sting taken out of their sails', he declared.

I gave a talk to a nurses' conference at the Sheraton-Wentworth. At the end of the evening, a South Australian nurse approached me and said compassionately, 'This must have been hell for you'. In what way, I wondered. 'You've been surrounded all night by women', she explained.

I recently met a man called Ashley Irwin. 'Surely he must come from South Australia', I said to myself. But no, he wasn't. I was flabbergasted.

I mentioned to a colleague that on a visit to Adelaide I didn't see any pretty girls in the street. 'That's nothing', he said, 'I lived there for a year and I didn't see any girls'.

Playing tennis in Fiji against a couple of South Australians on the morning of a tournament, I noticed that the sister of one, a lovely girl called Sarah, came to watch her brother play. I found this very touching, that Sarah should give up her time and stand under a tropical sun to encourage her brother. I was less than touched when I met Sarah's parents, however. 'Where do you two come from?' asked the mother. 'Queensland', said my partner. 'New South Wales', I confessed. 'I know you come from New South Wales', said the father, 'I heard you pronounce pool'. I wondered how this pharaoh pronounced it. 'Poule', he said. 'But that's the French for chook', I protested. He had the good grace to laugh and I decided that for a Crow-Eater he wasn't such a bad bloke. At least he had sired Sarah.

Comedy writers think they're going deaf when they go to Adelaide. Sure-fire laugh lines that have registered everywhere in the world are received in silence by the quiet-flowing Torrens.

Vineyard workers in South Australia were asked to wear rectal thermometers by the government. Local Health Minister, Dr John Cornwall, explained that it was part of a programme for testing heat stress, and that the thermometers were made of flexible plastic which was barely noticed a few minutes after insertion.

Singer Margaret Roadknight was heckled by radicals while

giving a concert in Adelaide. In response she coined the ultimate cause for them: Land Rights for Gay Whales.

South Australian sports commentator Ken Cunningham once made an astonishing admission. 'I'm not up to the hilt as far as soccer is concerned', he confessed.

Flautist James Galway has delighted audiences all around the world. The Adelaide critics were waiting for him, however, and he responded to this bucketing by challenging one of them to a duel. The Adelaide critic declined the offer.

The misunderstood Reg Livermore also got bad reviews for one of his shows (*Ned Kelly*) from the notorious Adelaide critics. 'I shouldn't have gone there', he said, 'it was like John F. Kennedy going to Dallas'.

Most people get stomach upsets when they go to Adelaide. This is because the water is unsafe to drink.

The managing director of the Adelaide Steamship Company, John Spalvins, was asked to name his hero. 'Anyone who works for wage restraint', said the wit and *bon viveur*.

A leading rock identity described Adelaide as 'Auckland without the excitement'.

Driving out of Adelaide on the last day of the Sheffield Shield decider between Victoria and South Australia in 1980, I followed match reports in between sighs of relief. Needing 234 to win, South Australia were 1 for 80-something when the hopelessly inefficient South Australian radio stations petered out. I later discovered from New South Wales radio that Victoria dismissed their folding opponents for 160 and won the Shield.

A South Australian theatre critic is known interstate as Cadbury. Why? Because he is a fruit and nut.

Many visitors contract viral infections in Adelaide. The disease is known as Light's Blight.

Sports Novels described South Australian Les Favell batting against Frank 'Typhoon' Tyson in this manner: 'He was like a sheep in a thunderstorm.'

I took my car to a car wash to get rid of the appalling red dust that plagues South Australia. Instead of an automatic three-minute machine, the 'car wash' consisted of a laborious hose-and-cloth job administered by a scruffy youth in jeans and gumboots. I went over to enquire if the car would be ready within the hour and caught sight of two superb breasts. The only beautiful girl in Adelaide was wearing jeans and gumboots and washing cars for a living.

SA Ombudsman Mary Beasley tried to get a free Qantas ticket for her 'live-in companion' Susan Mitchell. 'Susie and I are in a family situation', explained the Ombudsman.

Adelaide social worker Ms Debbie McClintoch wanted men banned from a seminar she was organising on 'Women and Work'. So she applied for help to the Anti-Discrimination Board of South Australia.

A 28-year-old woman appeared in the Port Adelaide Magistrates Court on 12 September 1983, on charges including the rape of a sixteen-year old youth.

In another reference to the declining male population, an Adelaide man described his home town as 'a city with lots of churches but no Chappells'.

At the opening night of Big River at the Adelaide Festival the intervals were half an hour long. This was so assorted Adelaide Bigwigs could meet the Governor-General.

The long history of sex-and-mutilation crimes, abductions and murders in South Australia is too sickening to contemplate.

The *Sydney Morning Herald* broke new ground when it

appointed Michael Le Moignan as its film critic. Mick is not a divorced female. He does not come from Adelaide.

At a party to announce the Playmate of the Year, *Playboy* pulled off the coup of the century. They engaged a comedian from Adelaide!

A female gynaecologist has a sign up in her Adelaide waiting-room which reads 'No smoking. No dogs. No men'.

In a cricket match at the MCG in 1981, Adelaide-born Greg Chappell instructed his brother, Adelaide-born Trevor Chappell, to bowl an underarm delivery.

In Western Australia a girl stole a kiss from Prince Charles. In Adelaide, on 5 April 1983, a woman stole a kiss from Princess Diana. Her name was Isabella.

An English friend of mine visited Adelaide for the first time. He was fascinated. The men there are so severely repressed, he said, much worse than the most psychologically crippled English public school man. Why should this be, he wondered. 'Did you meet any Adelaide women?' I asked.

Australian plays have always had a rough passage in Adelaide. The first Adelaide Festival was held in 1960 and they got off to a flying start by banning *The One Day of the Year*.

Marriage is such a rare experience for South Australian women that it's not surprising they get some things round the wrong way. When she married David Combe Meena Blesing retained her surname and changed her first name.

A sign outside the Adelaide Wine Cellar boasts 'We have the best quiche in town'.

A friend of mine was summoned to Adelaide by her sister because of a family crisis. It appeared that my friend's niece had 'embraced Sappho' and moved in with a woman who was a shop steward in a factory. 'It's not the homosexuality I object to', trilled the mother of the Sapphic one, 'It's just that she could have taken up with a better class of gel'.

Arriving at little-used Adelaide Airport in 1960, singer Johnny O'Keefe was asked by an interviewer, 'Do you think rock and roll is immoral?'

Following marital and political upheavals, lobbyist David Combe was given a new job. As an Australian Trade Commissioner in Vancouver, Combe welcomed the Prince and Princess of Wales to the Australian pavilion at Expo. 'What greater symbol of acceptability could there be,' he said, 'than shaking hands with the future King of Australia in British Columbia?'

J.I.M. Stewart said, in his capacity as Professor of English at Adelaide University, in 1940: 'I am most grateful to the Commonwealth Literary Fund for providing the funds to give these lectures in Australian literature, but unfortunately they have neglected to provide any literature. I will, therefore, lecture on D.H. Lawrence's *Kangaroo.*'

Barry Phillips-Moore, Don Candy and Broderick Dyke are South Australian tennis players.

In Adelaide in July 1986 a first grade footballer was suspended for three weeks. His transgression? Kissing the umpire.

Former South Australian premier Don Dunstan made the ultimate comment on his home state. He became Chairman of the Victorian Tourism Commission.

The 1984 New Zealand Rugby team defeated South Australia 99-0 in Adelaide. The tourists' coach, Bryce Rope, said he was not happy with his team's performance.

A friend of mine from Sydney was told four times on his first morning in Adelaide that South Australia had no convict origins.

'I felt as if I should massage my ankles and complain of hereditary chain soreness', he said.

An Adelaide medical scientist said in 1984 he hoped human beings would be able to reproduce asexually within the next hundred years.

When England played New Zealand in a limited-over cricket match at Adelaide Oval, the crowd vociferously supported England. When England played Australia the next day, crowd support of England dropped to 49 per cent.

'I think intelligent women who happen to be attractive really have some problems', said Robert Freak, the director of the Adelaide Centre of Personal Encounter.

Humphrey Bear is made in Adelaide. The Writers' Guild were horrified to learn that members were being paid $70 for a one-hour script. They advised an immediate raise. The local television chiefs had a meeting and emerged with a new offer: $85 a script. A strike ensued.

'Our Mother, who art in heaven . . .' is the new opening line of the Lord's Prayer being used at Adelaide's Annesley College.

Sue was from Adelaide, but I could hardly believe it. She had a lovely smile, and a calming influence on everyone around her. She created a happy work atmosphere and looked great in a swimsuit. She was bright, well spoken and kindly. Good on you, Sue.

Sports

If you drive past a suburban tennis court on a Saturday afternoon and see a game of doubles in progress, then the chances are those healthy, happy people are enjoying themselves in the fresh air. If there is someone sitting in the umpire's chair holding a clipboard, then the chances are those healthy, happy people are locked in the mortal combat that is competition tennis, a drama-game seemingly devised by Strindberg and Rafferty. Here follows a guide to its customs and rules.

Props

All along Avoca Street, Randwick, or Glenferrie Road, cars with cassettes blaring and racquets on the back seat can be seen every Saturday, driven by comp players in 'proper tennis attire'. A copy of the draw sheet will be on the passenger seat, together with some of the other props — gauze tape, vitamin E cream, a packet of Blizzards, a frozen Popper, bandaids, blockout, a radio, a stale towel and, in the case of one seasoned lady, a bottle of brandy ('She plays her best when she's halfway through it', says a team-mate).

Clubs

The biggest club in the eastern suburbs of Sydney is the Eastern Suburbs, in Dolphin Street, Coogee. This is the club which organises the coups in the area and holds the presentations at the end of them, in which teams book tables, bring their own nibbles, and cart off dreadful prizes.

One year all the prizes were identically cracked teak salad bowls, but more often you get seeming replicas of the pewter plate Dirk Hartog hammered up in WA in 1608. The only difference is that these plates would disintegrate if pierced by a nail. No one can say that materialism has spoiled the game at Easts.

As well as hosting presentation nights, the club has become something of ·a marriage market, with many players making their arrangements formal. Things are kept in perspective, however. 'When's the wedding?' my mixed partner asked a bride-to-be recently. 'Twenty-ninth of April', was the reply. 'But that's a Sunday', Janelle pointed out. 'That's right', said the unblushing one, 'we don't want the wedding to interfere with comp'.

Some of the singles don't go all the way, however. Two of them, in their thirties, were in the car park because the woman was buying the man's television set. I helped him carry it over to her car and then we squorbled it into the passenger seat of her car. Suddenly she changed her mind. The set was much bigger than she'd thought, it wasn't the right shape, she didn't want it, she'd furnished her flat just how she wanted it and this would ruin everything. The single man and I then lifted the set out of her car and started the long walk back across the car park.

Dedication

Cecilie, irredeemably pregnant, was coughing and retching in spasms on the floor of the hall. Her busband Les appeared. He stepped over her on his way out to play comp tennis. Says Cecilie: 'I'd do the same'.

Injuries

If you aren't carrying an injury or recovering from one then you are dead in comp tennis. You simply don't fit in. Black or white, male or female, you must have an injury. Backs and knees are most popular, but shoulders and feet are gaining more acceptance. It is also very popular to have taken up tennis after an injury in another sport. Kneeguards are the most effective method of getting this across. The implications are: 1. you were heading for the top in the other sport before fate cruelly intervened; 2. if you'd started tennis earlier in life you would have gone much further. Comp tennis is the great second-chance sport for ex-alcoholics, ex-footballers and the ex-young.

Umpires

Many people think of umpires as divisive forces in the game, but on at least one occasion a bad umpire proved to be a healing agent. One match I adjudicated, a competition mixed-doubles encounter, featured a husband-and-wife team who constantly bickered and sniped at each other, even when the ball was in play.

Sitting up in the umpire's chair wearing a cap and glasses, I stayed silent when one of my team's shots hit the baseline — or so I thought. The rally continued. The pair who had previously looked good things for the Family Court then started to abuse me, even though the ball was in play. Back and forth went the rally, and on and on went the abuse. The ball had been clearly out. I should pull my cap down over my head and jump off the chair. I needed binoculars, not glasses. And so it went.

I had no suitable comeback to this torrent, but noted one positive outcome. The couple were united, their differences forgotten, and had they come in a station wagon there was no telling how far the reconciliation would have gone.

Wearing glasses has often saved me from being called a cheat, and my shortcomings as an umpire have been rightly attributed to gross incompetence. An academic who plays comp doesn't wear glasses, however, and he was called a cheat. 'I can't be a cheat', he protested, 'I have a PhD in moral philosophy'.

Language

The language of comp tennis, as with most amateur mixed sports, is Suburban Genteel. You attend a match, where the time of commencement is usually one o'clock. You are correctly attired. The club provides amenities for its patrons. The secretary is invariably a wearer of spectacles. After a match has been completed the captain must forward payment to the hon. treas. Competitors who become deceased during a match will forfeit.

Handy phrases include:

Not up — the ball has bounced twice

I c-call 'em as I s-see 'em — the umpire's stout defence

Elect, to — choose or decide. In tennis you 'elect' to serve, 'elect' to go for the big one, and elect to stack a meeting in order to become president of the club.

Shift Work

I joined a club by looking through the local suburban rag's classified ads. There was one team, Alexandria, advertising for players to join, mainly because hardly anyone lives in Alexandria. It's an industrial suburb in the heart of Sydney and it's like a ghost town at the weekends when the factories are closed. The only life is provided by the cries and whispers of the comp players on Saturday afternoon. These players are a chequered group, with a high proportion of interstate people (the Melburnians, born politicians, get themselves on to the committee), New Zealanders, 'ethnics' (including one genuine punk Filipino), society types who go skiing and talk a lot about it, inner-city street-fighting types, a large proportion of single women aged about twenty-nine, a macho gay with a black dog, quite a few country people who've moved to the city and look a bit lost, Maoris with holes in their mufflers, bank girls called Sue, Karens who drive rusty Mazdas, and one playwright who thought he'd found a place where no one would know who he was (they twigged immediately).

The Role of the Minimally Talented Committee Person

The Minimally Talented Committee Person gravitates to the selection committee and puts himself in a team well above his standard. He surrounds himself with good players who are either junior stars shooting up or Obliging Types who never complain.

The juniors realise they'll be moving up soon, so they don't mind partnering a Minimally Talented Committee Person. The Obliging Types realise that the only way they can move is down so they shut up when the Minimally Talented Committee Person double faults on break point.

There are those who say that anyone who has to endure the boredom of committee meetings deserves a few perks and who is to say they're not right?

The Ladies

The tennis ladies range from flat-chested nationally-ranked twelve-year-olds right through the full bloom to diet fanatics in their fifties. Some of them can get out of a yellow Subaru wearing a tennis dress and make it memorable, while others realise it would be best for all concerned if they didn't get into a Subaru of any colour in the first place.

'Women's tennis is less conflictual than men's', said an earnest sociologist recently. Quite apart from the fact that there is no such word as 'conflictual', there is just as much conflict in women's tennis, although it is expressed in different ways. I don't pretend to understand all the eddies and currents of female conflict in the average tennis club, but the signs are all there, the smiling abuse, the bouts of 'no speaks', the descriptions of each other ('She's the one with the heavy hips'; 'If she turns around too quickly she gives herself a black eye') and some of the loaded conversations about clothes all add up to evidence that you don't have to shout abuse at the umpire to be 'conflictual'. It would be hard to convince an earnest sociologist of this, but it is my experience that there is just as much conflict in women's tennis as there is in men's. It just happens to be that sort of game, requiring the utmost in precision and concentration. Everyone falls short of this and everyone takes it out on everyone else.

White Death

The ladies serve afternoon tea on Saturday afternoon. They bring it and they make it. They pay less for the court than the men and they don't have to umpire. Occasionally a few male feminists raise their voices in protest about this arrangement, but the women keep mum. They know they've got a good deal and that's just how they want it. They're Ladies Who Want to be Ladies.

Since the health-food fads came in, afternoon tea tends to be short on white bread and white sugar. Sandwiches are made with wholemeal bread, and few get eaten, because no one likes wholemeal bread. One of the triumphs of the health-food movement is to get people to buy but not eat horrible-tasting things.

Man's Role

The male partner in mixed doubles is expected to 'put it away'. This means he is expected to pounce on any high ball and volley a clean winner. It's no good saying you 'go for depth' or you 'rely on placement'. Most, if not all, female partners will tell you to 'put it away'.

Anyone for Tennis?

I have never heard anyone in real life use this phrase. It originated in the twenties when bad playwrights needed an excuse to get a group of characters off stage in a hurry. Modern equivalent: 'Your parents are here'.

Courts

The courts in our comp range from the lurid artificial grass of Lyne Park, Rose Bay, with its beautiful harbour views, up to the lush dam valley of Cooper Park, where real eels swim in the stream and it is a far cry from the brown-green plains of White City.

Farther south, the arc takes in the Clovelly club, with a threatening cliff on one side and an authentic bellowing crone on the other. Astrolabe Park is a forlorn windswept prairie somewhere on the way to Botany, while the Pagewood Bus Depot is good old-fashioned sand with plenty of long grass for the veterans to lose the ball in while they regain their breath.

Alexandria has the best courts — flawless cement with a bounce you can stake your life on — but the setting, a sleeping industrial landscape, is not inspiring.

There used to be one long river of courts from Vaucluse to Cronulla, but now space is precious and the remaining ones encourage the volleyer — there isn't much room behind the baseline and a cross-court shot at Clovelly will hit the cliff before you can move.

The Nightmare

Large numbers of New Zealanders have migrated to Australia in recent years. 'They've raised the IQ of both countries', said Robert Muldoon. They've also lowered the number of videos in residential areas, as more than a few New Zealanders have got themselves involved in the drugs-and-crime scene.

There was one Souths team that was full of Maoris. They were nice people. You could lend them your front-door key and the video would be safe. They probably didn't live in Bondi and probably didn't hang towels over the front balcony. They were pretty musclebound, however, and they wore kneeguards and used a lot of topspin. 'You wouldn't want to face them on a fast court on a cold day with a gale blowing and the odd shower of rain', I said (or something like that) after we beat them on our slow courts on a still, warm day.

The nightmare came true. And of course we lost. And we got cold and wet and pulled muscles on the slippery court. 'At least we now know why those Maoris wear kneeguards', I said as I limped off the court.

21   Social Cricket Manoeuvres

The Nucleus

The nucleus of a social cricket team numbers about six. It is the job of the secretary to find the other five from week to week out of a field of about forty. One year my team merged with another team which also had a nucleus of six. 'Now we'll have a nucleus of twelve', I beamed. I was wrong. That year we had a nucleus of six.

The Big Gun Theory

Most social cricket manoeuvres revolve around the perceived strength of the opposition. One year my team, the Metros, took the ill-advised step of entering a shipping company knockout competition. In our first match we came up against a team from Stephenson Pty Ltd. This was a fairly ragged-looking outfit with a left-hander in denim shorts, a girl called Brenda, and so on. But the Stephenson who led the team was the boss's son and he was a fast bowler who had played a bit of first grade. Someone had forgotten the mats and on a pock-marked malthoid 'pitch' we were lucky to escape with a mere defeat. Stephenson junior had hit up a 50 against us, and we were all quite dry-eyed when his broad and expensive bat was stolen later in the afternoon.

The counter to the Big Gun is often the Long Lunch, and our opposition one grey and threatening day, the G.D. Barnard XI, disappeared for more than ninety minutes. After the Long Lunch, as the black clouds glided in from the south, the opposition batsmen slowly made their way out to the crease to open the innings like actors on the second night of a flop. They were hopelessly behind on run rate when the rain set in and we left the only perfect wicket we have ever played on. There were a few backward glances at the beautiful green plot and more than a few ruminations later over a couple of beers to the effect that maybe the G.D. Barnard XI doesn't get beaten because they don't get beaten.

I have had a particular aversion to the use of the Big Gun ever since I bowled to Bobby Simpson one day and received a terrible caning. The gap between social cricket and the more heady heights is vast, and I could never understand the mentality of that species of hoon, the first-grader who turns out for a Sunday game in the park. Some of them even take delight in beaning a number eleven batsman who is patently somebody's brother-in-law. Live and learn is a good philosophy, however, and next time we come up against a Big Gun you can bet we'll head off to Chinatown at lunchtime for a nine-course yum cha.

The Friday Night Renege

Club secretaries dread the gambit whereby the opposition secretary rings and offers to cancel two days before the event. 'Too many of our blokes are unavailable', he says helplessly. You protest, refer to your burgeoning phone bill, say you've gone to a lot of trouble over this game, and your team will be murderously disappointed at having to cancel at such a late date. The apologetic opposition secretary then goes away to 'scratch up a few deadheads', you relax, and then get whacked by a team of superstars on the Sunday.

The Foot Soldiers

I have never understood that peculiar breed of social cricketer known as the Foot Soldiers. These poor helots will turn out for a team that has five good all-rounders. These five do all the bowling. When the team bats they either win by seven wickets or are 3 for something inadequate when the overs are up. The Foot Soldier never bats or bowls. At the end of the day's play he has a few beers and talks about either the catch he took or the catch he missed. An empire can be built on the sweat of the Foot Soldier, but he never gets any of the glory.

Pose and Counterpose

Sport has replaced opera as the platform for posers (I have dropped the 'u' from poseur, not wishing to appear a poser; besides, everyone in Bondi Junction pronounces it 'poser'). Parks and gardens are the places to be seen, walking the dog or wearing Tretorn tennis shoes. If you pedal around the bike tracks on your wife's rusty Cyclops with three-speed gears wearing cutdown jeans, then you are clearly inferior to someone on a twelve-speed Gitanes, wearing a crash helmet and stretch knickerbockers. Carry a tennis racquet and you jump several points, however. You ride a bike, sure, but only on the way to play a *real* sport. The ultimate sporting pose would probably involve swimming across the Harbour with a pair of football boots between your teeth.

Social cricket can be a minefield of poses, too. Who will forget Adelaide actor Ed Pegge's first appearance for our humble Metros? Ed arrived with a vinyl-covered Esky filled with smoked goose and white burgundy. He had a Lord's Taverners cap and a $200 bat in a zippered case. This was only superseded by his second appearance for us, wearing a white jacket with the legend 'ED PEGGE' emblazoned in red across the back. 'Damn fool thing', Ed dismissed it, 'we had to wear them at Lord's for the blasted TV cameras'.

Television producers Gary Reilly and Tony Sattler (RS Productions) booked the Don Bradman Oval at Bowral for a game. Unfortunately the fence there doesn't reach the ground, so that every time someone hit a boundary the ball shot away down one of the main steets of Bowral. Tourists must have thought we were part of some posey act to publicise the Don's home-town as we pursued the rolling ball along the bitumen and dodged the tooting cars.

Actor Terry 'Something's come up, Don' Bader was a master of the front-on pose. At a recent game, one of our team arrived victorious from an A-grade competition tennis match and took the field wearing his sweaty Ivan Lendl shirt of ringed diamonds. TB left him for dead, however. He wore a hat several sizes too big for him, and every time it fell off you could see the legend 'BOB WILLIS' next to the 9¾ size label. 'Bob gave it to me', explained Bader simply. Many of us were curious about the blue tent he was wearing. It looked as if a piece of sky had fallen and enveloped him. It turned out to be the one-day shirt Willis had worn on the 1982-83 tour. It was another gift from his mate Bob. Our feat of inveigling Bob's brother Dave to play for us paled visibly, especially when it transpired that Terry's mate Bob and half the MCC team had gone to see him and Kate Fitzpatrick in an *avant-garde* Canadian play and stayed to the end.

The Pocket Battleship

Playing against the (not so) Old Cranbrookians I was not looking forward to bowling at the tall Somerset batsman Peter Roebuck, the Big Gun we weren't expecting. During a break I was asked for my autograph by a small nineteen-year-old. Later he hit me for two consecutive sixes and won the match before Roebuck was needed.

One time we were saddled with a Mystery Pipsqueak by someone who had to drop out. He was definitely a brother-in-law type by the look of him. When the Mystery Pipsqueak went out to bat at number eleven we needed 24 off 4 balls to win. As he took guard there were some jocular remarks about his tiny stature and high-pitched voice. The first ball he received was hit for six over long-off. So was the second. Just before he was caught off the next ball we believed we were going to win. After he took off his pads we never saw this Pocket Battleship again. Such is the stuff that cricket dreams are made of.

Libels and Libations

One evening in the dry autumn of 1978 I was in England watching the embers of a village cricket match and having a few beers as guest of one of the captains and it struck me how friendly and civilised it all was. Some of the vilest hatreds that Australians bear for one another can be born or developed on the cricket field. As I remarked to my host, 'It's always much nicer when the captains don't sue each other for libel'.

A team we played called Forest Lodge was based at the famous Sydney University Hotel and contained some of the biggest drinkers I've ever seen in action. Before and since most of them have become prominent in law, politics and education. We had some exciting Ashes-style series against them (by exciting I mean we always won 3-2) and socialised quite a lot. The wives and children of my players came to the games and had a marvellous time. The female cohorts of the opposition appeared sporadically, but there wasn't much mixing between the Real Women on our side and the Gas Pumpers on the other. Only one of the opposition had a wife and children. Looking back on it, many of the fissures and tensions of the seventies were present at the innocent fields in Centennial Park where we played.

The crunch came in 1978 when one of the opposition sued me for libel, claiming that one of the characters in my play *Makassar Reef* was based on him and implied that he was fond of a drop. Had the play been a documentary account of his cricket career I could have understood the motives for litigation. As it was, I was puzzled but relieved when the case was dropped. It meant the end of the series with Forest Lodge, which was just as well as they had resorted to the Big Gun Theory by including a first-grader in a desperate attempt to beat us.

At the beginning of 1979 we played the 729 Club and were unmercifully thrashed by a team containing luminaries like ABC commentator Jim Maxwell. His mother had introduced my parents to each other but here was he, with little sense of history, hitting me over mid-off for four in a way that no one at Forest Lodge would have ever thought of. To compound the agony, my fellow playwright Bob Ellis dropped some hot chances in the gully. Ellis was often a figure of fun, with razors, little black books and condoms dropping out of his pockets on to the pitch during the precious few seconds of his life spent running between wickets. But he had a safe pair of hands in the gully for balls of the sort of velocity Forest Lodge was capable of.

This game was in every way a turning-point. We then sacked

Ellis and players of similar dress and girth, cut out drinking until after the game, got ourselves into long whites and recruited some good players, nearly all of them non-smokers. We also got a new kit and started practising at the nets.

Stepping up several echelons, we moved into a circuit where we have remained ever since and have enjoyed our cricket enormously, especially the day in 1982 when we thrashed the 729 Club. And all because of a libel suit.

Princes of Darkness

We've played a few curly teams over the years. There was Lenin's Eleven, a team of communists without a captain which arrived at all of its decisions democratically (and tardily). The GA World XI did not believe in conventional names, only initials, so we had to contend with the likes of GA, KD, TB and KFA (who came from Adelaide).

But of all the curly ones, the London Hotel was the most nearly concentric. They were a bunch of roisterers and drunks that virtually every team we knew stopped playing against. But we persisted in playing these recidivists mainly because of the extreme pleasure we got from beating them. (They enjoyed beating us too, considering us a mob of needlessly sober prigs.)

The first time we played them on a Good Friday it had been a lovely clear morning. In the afternoon we were moving towards victory when the opposition started lengthening the drinks breaks. It was a lovely fine autumn night as our last three wickets fell. We only knew they had fallen by the sound of the stumps being hit out there in the April gloom.

The next Good Friday we beat them by 8 runs in a certified thriller. The noise level had risen to an almost unbearable level as they coasted along towards our modest total of 86. Their last two wickets fell at 78, however, and we walked off the field to reverberating silence.

The third Good Friday they rose again and we had a tied score as the last over started. The London Hotel captain then instructed the umpire to call 'no ball' at the next delivery so his team could win by one wicket. Our bowler, Louis Nowra, overheard this and bowled from a metre behind the crease. The umpire called 'no ball' and the London Hotel won by one wicket. We wish them well in their search for someone to play against.

The Mean Machine

Playwright Louis Nowra and his wife Sarah were ornaments to our game until they inexplicably packed up and moved to South Australia. I urged them to allow South Australia's population to run down naturally but they wouldn't listen and flew off into the maelstrom of their own free will.

While they were with us Louis took an enormous number of wickets — far more than anyone else — with his Derek Underwood-style biters. 'Biters' seems more apt than spinners for this original type of slow-medium delivery that is midway between spin and seam. It always galled Louis, however, that I topped the bowling averages with my tidy medium pace. Sarah, our scorer, would set out the book like a Schoenberg musical score and, with her black fine-point pen and pocket calculator, we soon had a scorebook that would have graced a coffee-table or an auction at Sotheby's. Louis would stand looking over her shoulder and swear under his breath when my bowling figures were pointillised at their usual 2 for 18.

Louis was very competitive and temperamental (the more easygoing Ellis used to call him 'Anton Gundagai') and he was determined to supplant me at the top of the bowling averages. Having only one good eye was an advantage to him in his quest as he could drop catches off my bowling without attracting suspicion. The season wore on and he was beating my uninspiring 2 for 18 in match after match.

At the end of our last encounter, on a clear and windless Good Friday, he stood at the faithful Sarah's shoulder — her integrity holding up beautifully under the strain — and she tapped away at her machine and wrote down the season's figures as the sun set. Finally it was down there in black and green before our eyes — Buzo 7.9 and Nowra 9.8. Louis was furious; Sarah looked vaguely guilty but managed a graceful autumnal smile as she looked around at the expectant faces. I then accepted lukewarm congratulations from some of the team.

Several beers later, when I got home, I took out the scorebook
and flicked back through Sarah's baroquery. Sure enough, there
was a mistake. Sarah had credited me with taking an uncharac-
teristic and fanciful 3 for 4. Did I ring the Nowras and report that
my claim to the throne was invalid? No, they went to Adelaide in
a fittingly sombre mood.

Locales and Locals

The most favoured arenas are the turf wickets at Centennial
Park. Here where the sight screen is a flock of red kites and the
leg-spinners pitch in the hoof marks you can shoulder arms to a
wide and still be bowled. People stream across the field, oblivious
of the twenty-two figures watching them with hands on hips.

Women who sound like FM radio announcers from Adelaide
walk dogs from fine leg to backward point; Italian families stroll
genially behind the bowler's arm; punks lie down at long-off to
dry out in the sun; a beautiful lady in a dented Saab — according
to legend — occasionally stops to watch.

Amazingly, most games finish on time, and involve such
forgotten cricket arts as batting on a sticky wicket. (The day the
pitches are covered in Centennial Park is the day they put muzak
in traffic lights.) On a good day, however, when the sky is a time-
less blue and the Moreton Bay fig trees look like frozen lyrebirds
there can't be many better places to be. It's certainly more toney
than Camperdown Oval, an overpriced chook yard in an urban
smellorama. (We've never won at Camperdown Oval.)

There are definite strata in Sunday cricket. Generally speaking, the good teams will have ten players in white. For some reason I have never seen a team all in white. Lower down the ladder
the 1970 track suits and stubbies start to creep in, and then the
can at square leg, the singlets and cigarettes, the swaying
umpires and malthoid pitch right through to the dogs in the slips
and the little piles of ice.

Rogues Gallery

Opponents our team has come up against in the gruelling world of Sunday cricket have included most walks of life but very few walkers. International bankers Paul Nankivell and Murray Sime are never out; when they take a wicket they feel the batsman should turn out his pockets to them. Midnight-to-dawn radio announcer Tim Ritchie sticks by his decisions with a furious, bleary-eyed moral force. His 2JJJ colleague Mac Cocker has an all-or-nothing approach: he feels all the decisions should go his way and nothing else.

Some mighty duels have taken place out in the griddle. Who will forget the fate of the burly Macca, scorer of too many fifties for Forest Lodge against us? He was caught in the gully for a duck by Bob Ellis in one game, and I put Ellis there again next game when Macca came in. There was a bit of sledging along the lines that Macca was Ellis's bunny. Macca affected a hollow laugh and looked around contemptuously at the (then) frail figure of Ellis. First ball he received he was caught by Ellis.

Macca didn't play in the next match. He was rumoured to have withdrawn to a religious retreat on the North Coast, there to brood awhile. Later on in his life he became a rugby coach.

Finishing Tight

Occasionally the cried of 'Fix!' or 'Stew!' echo through the green mantles of social cricket. At the Reg Bartley Oval, parked among the camphor laurels and storm-water channels of Rushcutters Bay, Writers played Publishers in a recent needle match. The Publishers made 202 and the Writers appeared to be hacking it with solid innings from television scriptos Greg Haddrick and Chris Fitchett. There was a collapse in the prose department, however, when Bradman biographer Jack Egan went for a duck — no doubt a clever spoof of his idol's last test appearance.

Sundowners Jon Cleary and Trevor Shearston managed only five between them, but the tail wagged and with the sight of Bob Ellis padded up in the twilit pavilion to spur us on, we got to 200 with one ball to come. This was hit for two and the match was a tie. No, we didn't land any new publishing contracts, just a Toohey's or two to celebrate the result.

The *Playboy* magazine XI were a different proposition. They drank beer, sure, but it was Heineken. They arrived early and beavered away setting up their monogrammed marquee. In the end they had to score five runs off the last five balls to snatch a win. Their associate editor was the man with the bat but he missed all five deliveries with desperate airswings — or airbrushes, as someone said. Wives in see-through tops gathered under the marquee and watched the lads go down in a match they were always going to win.

Characters, Too

I always thought the ultimate cricket achievement would involve long innings. That was until I saw actor Terry Bader skulking under the trees during a cricket match. 'I've got to stay pale', explained TB, 'I'm playing an Englishman in the *Bodyline* series'. This dedicated artist then got out selflessly for a duck and hurried back under the trees.

Professional reputations or images don't mean everything when you turn out for a Sunday game. Left-wing MLA Rod Cavalier belied his name when he held us up for hours on the mats at Haberfield. Earlier that season we thrashed a team containing several of the stars of the *Bodyline* series. Les Dayman, who plays wicketkeeper Bert Oldfield, bowled like a demon. John Waters, founder member of Lord's Taverners (Australia), has a batting average that viewers of *Playschool* could work out. Sociology Professor Bob Connell has often turned bowlers into a disadvantaged sub-culture with some élitist input from his bat. *Sixty Minutes* producer Alan Hogan, however, typified his hangdog breed by turning out with a headache and bare feet. We got him for a duck, and there weren't any more of these stories.

Thank Heaven

My advice to any fledgling social cricket captain would be this: Don't put men of religion in the slips. I am not suggesting that Bobby Simpson and Ian Chappell are necessarily pagans; rather,

I am passing on empirical evidence that the slips is the place for agnostics or spasmodic church-goers. I had been amused to read of Freddie Trueman's comment to the Rev. David Sheppard when the minister dropped yet another catch off his bowling: 'Ar come on, Rev. You've had enough practice putting your hands together'. When we played a game on the Monday of a holiday weekend we were a bit short so one of our regulars brought along his brother, an Anglican deacon who hadn't been able to play with us previously because 'Sunday's his big day'. I put the deacon in the slips. When he dropped a simple catch from one of the openers I didn't think much of it. When the opener was on 69 and they needed two runs to win I have to admit the incident crossed my mind as I bowled. The opener cracked what we all thought was a winning boundary but the ball didn't get there. It had been sensationally caught at short mid-wicket by the deacon's brother, a classical guitarist. 'How are the hands?' I asked him. 'I don't know', he said, 'I can't feel them'. He then closed his eyes in what was definitely not a transport of religious ecstasy.

Years later I still had not learned my lesson when I put a lay preacher from St Mark's in the slips. Two dropped catches later he was on the fine leg boundary and I had learned my lesson. In fairness I ought to point out that both men were excellent batsmen who were able to play long innings unfazed by the unusually high number of lives they had.

Great Expectations

'Scratch your arse but don't tear the skin', said a cricket coach to the young Les Dayman when asked the right tempo for an about-to-be-launched innings. As the incident took place in Adelaide the imagery was predictable, but I think it wonderfully eloquent, too. Dayman's understanding of this example of cricket colloquiala was that he should keep the score ticking over, which he would have done had he not been out first ball. Amateur cricket is truly the palace of dreams.

22 Polo Vaulting

*A*rriving at Warwick Farm for the Australian Open Polo Series is rather like driving into a giant outdoor living-room. Here among the moleskins and Volvos, the serene gums and mellowing poplars, there is a friendly rural gentility that is not to be sneered at.

The PA system is quietly tuned to the ABC, which on Sunday mornings is like Musak with all the rough edges taken off. The midday news comes on and the siege of Mount Panorama is calmly related.

Lazing in the sun among the Rovers and the bottles of Noilly Prat and the pâté being served from the boot, we hear of rioting bikies throwing cans full of gravel and lighting fires, of ninety-one arrests for drunkenness and assault. There are forty policemen at Warwick Farm, but they are here to play music.

In some circles polo is regarded as an esoteric mating ritual for the aristocracy, where the odd Rhodesian accent can be heard. It is certainly that, and anyone with an aversion to check shirts, pipes, and card tables full of champagne should continue to stay away. If they do they will miss a fast and intermittently exciting sport played in a relaxing ambience.

As the yobs and can-throwers continue their take-over of cricket, motor-racing and most codes of football, the indelibly middle-class sports like softball and polo are starting to come into their own.

The typical day brings two matches of twenty-three-goal polo. Each player has a handicap from one for beginners to ten for the top brass. At present, forty-goal polo (i.e. all four players on a team have handicaps of ten) is only played in Argentina. The average grafter, such as Prince Philip or Prince Charles, has a handicap of three.

So twenty-three-goal polo is not too bad a standard and it makes for good viewing as the teams gallop up and down the prairie-like arena (300 yards by 200 yards) in pursuit of the round grail.

Ideally the ball is made from willow roots, but in this case is plastic, and quickly declines from a radiant white sphere to a wizened rhomboid as the riders whirl their mallets and crack it towards the distant goal.

Quite often they miss. Timing is difficult on the canter and there is also (especially to rugby-bred eyes) the scrappiness endemic to all the 'offside' games — soccer, hockey and Australian Rules. But any feeling that polo is for the delicate or the effete is dispelled by the shoulder-charging and hell-bent galloping that ebbs and floods throughout the six chukkas (seven and a half minutes each) of the match.

As the chukkas mount I get used to the pattern of play. Over on the far side it is difficult to see what is happening and one is vaguely reminded of a querulous group of centaurs playing marbles for money.

When they charge the near side the spectators keep a self-preserving eye on the ball, as it sometimes bullets across the sideline and into the card tables. The sight of up to eight horses earthquaking straight at them causes justifiable flutters among some of the older ladies and 100 per cent of the playwrights in the audience.

They always stop in time, however, and straddle off the sideline barrier with arrogant dexterity. The horses are trained to muster sheep and then to play polo and can stop on a sixpence or follow the ball without any guide from the reins.

There is a lot of close marking in defence, notably from Howard Hipwood, an eight-goal professional from Britain and the gun player (on paper) of the circuit. To overcome this, many shots are lofted and some are intended to blaze some kind of trail through the ruck.

'The ball didn't get through — it hit a couple of ponies on the head', reported the commentator unemotionally at one stage. The horse ambulance is called for after one incident, but the animal is only dazed and the organisers are quick to point out that serious injuries are rare and that the (unquoted) horses love the game.

During the stoppage the sponsors extract their dues with low-key un-Packer painlessness. The Pacific resort of Soqulu is described with factual romanticism (strange and beautiful tropical fish, nine-hole golf course). The programme thanks the Beneficial Finance Corporation for its support and notes objectively that the advent of sponsorship 'Was not unlike the revolution which occurred in cricket about the same period, except that the organisers of our sport have had much greater control over the changes that have taken place'.

The organisers claim their sport is the 'fastest ball game in the world' and are keen to impress their slogan 'Polo for the people' on everyone. They are also proud of the doubling of Sydney's polo fields in the eighties, and plan for a future as a major sport, alongside cricket and football, and with just as big a following. Where will these spectators come from? I quote a report from the Planning and Environment Commission: pony clubs constitute the most popular worldwide sport among young people.

If polo is poised to move in beside cricket and football, then it is to be hoped that none of what distinguishes it from those yob-dominated sports will be lost, for many of polo's virtues are to be found outside the playing arena, in the unpolluted charm of the setting. There are no slags, no barracking, and the few cans end up in the rubbish bin.

Some of these people may be descendants of Captain de Groot's New Guard, but at least you can ignore them without reprisals. On the Hill at the Sydney Cricket Ground the yobs won't allow you that luxury. If you ignore them they'll throw cans at you. I am talking, by the way, about the Hill in the eighties. No one believes me when I tell them that swearing was never heard on the Hill in the fifties. It was no garden party, of course, but there was a definite standard of good behaviour and the phrase 'Ladies present' used to mean something.

The reduction of the yobs to radio statistics is something to be welcomed by the polo crowd after the trauma of the Bong Bong Picnic Races. Here the aristos and the yobs are thrown together chic by jowl and it does not work out all that well. A friend of mine said the most shaky fingers he ever saw were those of a hotelier near Bong Bong locking up his property on the morning of the races before fleeing to the coast along with half the town. Apparently the flight of the Huguenots had nothing on this.

Polo, along with business, brothels and the royal family, is very much back in favour and you can't help wondering if this isn't a reaction against the descent of the left into violence and lunacy. Perhaps in the future the act of buying a ticket for the polo will reveal many characteristics about the buyers and their aspirations. One of them will be a vote against the Bong Bong Yobboes. If the New Class has spoilt things for the intelligentsia, then surely the yobs have blown it for the proletariat.

23 On First Learning that Norths Have Signed Olsen Filipaina

Much have I travelled in the realms of League,
And seen them all from Pearce to McTigue;
Round many verdant ovals have I been
Whose oft-banged fences are blood to our screen.
Of one stout army I hear nought but ill:
A fiefdom where Lucifer would fit the bill.
Yet did I ne'er sup with elongated spoon
Till of Olsen I heard from Mercury's platoon;
Then felt I like some diver of the deep
When a medic reveals with nary a peep
That testosterone levels have been sapped and slowed.
O brave Cortez knew without being specific
To stay above and well clear of the Pacific
And kick the round balls of a different code.
(With apologies to 'On First Looking into Chapman's Homer' by John Keats)

Results

24 The Grand Mixmaster

Catamaran 80

While virulent publicity has been accorded the Australian Indoor Tautology Pennant, in which contestants like Norman May speak of 'vacant gaps' and the like, another tournament has been quietly garnering adherents among those who fail to see any entertainment value in throwing cans at Norman May. I refer to the Grand Mixmasters Invitational.

More akin to croquet and badminton, the GMI is held aboard a frigate anchored off the southern Tasmanian town of Catamaran in the middle of winter. This comparative isolation — with due respect to the non-floating population of Catamaran — tends to discourage undesirable elements.

Who participates in this exclusive event? Invitees must be people of sound character and private means who have mixed their metaphors in public. The patron saint of the GMI is the late Hollywood film producer Sam Goldwyn, whose statements included: 'You've got to take the bull between the teeth' and 'The trouble with these directors is they're always biting the hand that lays the golden egg'.

Goldwyn's baton was picked up by director Michael Curtiz, who kept the flame alive in the factory of dreams when he said to a cinema proprietor who specialised in horror films: 'When I see the pictures you play in that theatre it makes the hair stand on the edge of my seat.'

The torch was borne adrift in the post-war years by political journalist Ian Fitchett, who described the predicament of a prominent public servant: 'In the corridors of power he was always in the eye of the storm'.

And so to the present. Distinguished and frequently hyphened guests in white tie and ball gown were piped aboard the seagull-festooned HMAS *Swansea*. They came by yacht; and helicopter, some by primitive outboard or dinghy, but they all had one thought in mind: free *hors d'oeuvre* and champagne for starters.

Below decks, in the opulently appointed dressing rooms for the invitees (not just anyone could enter), the excitement was running high as the first shot was struck by new chum Nigel Starmer-Smith, the BBC Rugby man, who said: 'At Murrayfield Scotland play France. Both teams are without a win and both will be trying to stave off the spectre of the wooden spoon.'

What a splendid effort by this enterprising chap! It put him on the first rung of the table with another visiting entrant, the American favourite, the *Charlotte, NC, Observer* 'Judith Guest . . . Marilyn French . . . Elizabeth Forsyth Hailey. These names, during the last three years, have risen like night vapours from the flat fields of obscurity to etch our hearts and minds with the indelible ink of their powerful first novels.'

But what of the home front? Incipient despair was cut short by the pithy Federal politician, Mr Ralph Hunt, who swung a barb at NSW Health Minister, Mr Kevin Stewart. 'The ball is at Mr Stewart's feet. If he is genuinely concerned about health insurance rates, he will bite on the bullet and seriously examine this alternative concept in health care.'

Another ball was at the feet of a Rugby League player who toed it into the goalmouth during a Tooth Mug game. Needing only to fall on the ball for a try, he fell on the grass instead, causing genial compere Ray Warren to exclaim: 'What a time to drop all your lollies, when the world's your oyster!'

Not to be outgunned, rival compere Rex Mossop added a new string to his bow with an imaginative foray into atmospheric zeitgeist: 'Trains are cockle-doodle-dooing past us here at Lidcombe Oval.'

It was only fitting that the quality press should lend a dollop of tone to the proceedings by getting in for their chop with a couple of boomers. It was the *National Times* which saved the bacon of the weekly flagships: 'The first seeds of disaster for Melbourne as the financial heart came in the 1890s when the city's banking industry was badly scarred by the land bubble burst.' — Robert Gottliebsen.

'The basic structure of Australian universities is feudal, with the vice-chancellor at the apex, rather like a prince in the Holy Roman Empire . . .' – Dennis Altman.

The new respectability was maintained by Ian Manning, a gentleman of the turf, in a moving yet buoyant description of a long night's journey into day undertaken by Mr Tommy Hill: 'It has been a long time between drinks for the veteran trainer, but the light at the end of the tunnel finally shone through yesterday.'

Veteran theatre critic H.G. Kippax, who had laid many bets at the Old Tote, took a punt and kicked off by describing the Nimrod Theatre's production of *A Comedy of Errors* as: 'A gallimaufrey of unalloyed delight.'

While pondering how the unmixable could be mixed. I went for a walk around the ward. As the guests mingled in the Blue Emerald Room, Hobart was burnt for their entertainment and applejack was served in steaming beakers of sandstone. Potted palms were stuffed into portholes by members of the younger set, but they were decked by this broadside from Lionel Bowen, MHR: 'We can expect to see the current spate of appointments accelerated as the ship begins to go down and Mr Fraser's friends and colleagues move in to mop up the crumbs'.

Mr Bowen was referring to the Government's propensity towards granting sinecures to aficionados in contrast to the previous government's scandalous 'jobs for the boys' programme. But he was misunderstood by many of the guests.

The band played 'Nearer My God to Thee' as guests crammed loosely into a lifeboat. 'It's only a mixed metaphor', cried the captain of the *Swansea*, but the cream of the evening were rowing away from what they believed to be a sinking ship. As they headed for the gunwales of Catamaran, they were racked and bleached by a rising tide of seagull abuse.

Meanwhile, in the tournament proper, it was back to taws, down on the nitty-gritty. Politicians in the Invitational were keeping their 'options open', while sportscasters hoped they could 'make an incursion and go perilously close' to winning the joust. The critics found it all 'needed more depth in the relationships' but it was 'funny and touching' nevertheless. Some even vowed to stop writing (Meryl Streep) in or out of brackets every second line.

Only two were chosen for the dice with infinity. Rex Mossop and H.G. Kippax made a stirring mixed double as they fired off their coats into the ring. At a crucial stage in a Rugby League match, Mr. Mossop told his viewers: 'Canterbury have got Manly on the rack and they're screwing their tails.'

In reviewing Derek Jacobi's *Hamlet*, H.G. Kippax was a man overboard. His ecstasy reached its peak when he proclaimed: 'Mr Jacobi is Gielgud's successor, building from many parts a whole. And he proclaims his succession with most miraculous organ — in tones trumpet-tongued, or in a whisper.'

We had hardly time to ponder the advisability of getting an organ to sound like a trumpet when a boarding party from Catamaran started swarming all over the decks.

'We've heard enough!' shouted the leader of these vigilantes and, without further ado, HMAS *Swansea* was razed to the plimsoll line.

As I swam towards the embers of Hobart I recalled the enthusiasm that the siting of the GMI had aroused among the quarter-masters of Catamaran.

'They led us up the garden path and stabbed us in the back', I reflected, and clutched at a piece of driftwood (Meryl Streep).

Peron 81

There is no question that among Australian sporting events the Grand Mixmasters Invitational has not achieved the prominence of its rival, the Australian Indoor Tautology Pennant. The latter event has attracted more well-known celebrities, such as Don McLean, who sang eloquently of 'Faces going round and round in circular rotation'.

Mr Malcolm Fraser also lent his name and office to the proceedings with 'It's very hard to talk about the average Australian because most people are either above the average or below it'.

But what of the Mixmasters? Many of the sporting public do not know that in this competition media figures reap the wild surf by mixing their metaphors. Mr Neville Wran became an early patron of the Invitational when he discussed his strategy

for the 1976 election campaign: 'The welcome mat is not out for
federal politicians — we think they might prove to be a bit of lead
weight in our saddle-bags'.

Despite such star quality, the tournament has never really
etched itself into the tide of public acclamation. Some believe that
choice of venue could have something to do with it. Last year the
Invitational took place on a frigate anchored off the southern
Tasmanian town of Catamaran.

This year the suggested sites included Fremantle during the
America's Cup; at a 'Welcome Home' reception for the Australian test cricket team; at Liberal Party headquarters on election
night; and the obvious winning choice — Peron Island, off the
Northern Territory coast near Rum Jungle during the monsoon.

In their wisdom, the organisers of the Grand Mixmasters
decided not to waste money on promotion. The chief spokesman,
a Mr S.C.G. Hoodoo, said, 'We have a quality product, a desirable
venue, a targettable audience catchment of millions, and as far
as we're concerned it's a case of shut the gate and bolt the horse
on the distaff side of midnight; we have tossed our soft options
into the too-hard basket'.

This was good fighting stuff, and the campaign began in
earnest when press releases were sent out two days after the
event, and the show got under way two hours before the
advertised start. Telephone bookings, it was announced, would
be taken by Mr Lyon on (02) 969 2295. Admission was fixed at
$100 a head ($2000 a head for party bookings) but when both
spectators arrived they discovered that there was no box office,
just a few prisoners of the socialist left leaning on a spittoon and
waving them in for nothing.

Previewed by a goggle of television critics, the Invitational
was variously described by them as 'good escapist fare', 'mildly
shocking fare' and 'superior fare for the discerning viewer'.
Several of them, however, went to the pub halfway through the
fare.

Nevertheless, the Mixmasters got under way and very soon
reputations were being dented like a snowball on the back
burner. We began to sip the heady wine of the doldrums when
theatre critic Romola Costantino gushed over a revue called
Squirts: 'Squirts is something of a fizzer'.

She was followed into the fray by barnacled *Sixty Minutes* anchor-man George Negus, who stooped to this: 'The authorities are bending over backwards to keep a low profile'.

Cricket commentator Henry Blofeld took the new ball and raised a few eyebrows when he pulled down a screamer: 'But, if Brearley — who has his supporters — is to come back, the selectors might have to go on their knees to persuade him, which would be unsatisfactory and in any event his appointment could hardly be seen as a forward step'.

Blowers was aced out of the running by an unidentified grazier on ABC TV's *A Big Country*, who cut out the bull and told it straight about a wayward colleague: 'He backed the wrong horse — he bred cattle instead of buffalo'.

Sandra 'Dairymaid' Jobson milked a few stories for a few laughs when she waylaid Margaret Thatcher's husband's fears that he was getting old and shabby: 'Never mind, Denis, the Brits like things a bit scruffy behind the ears'.

Miss Jobson then stung the knockers with further news: 'That waspish New York theatre critic Clive Barnes pulled no punches when he reviewed Richard Burton's second debut on Broadway in *Camelot* last week'.

It was left to a journalist on the *Australian* to get the Murdoch flagship airborne. Mr Graeme Beaton creamed his way through the Dardanelles of oblivion when he took a punt on a falling star: 'The spectre of a chronic oil shortage through the present unpredictable chain of events which eventually, inevitably, sprang a trap for America's Ambassador to the UN, Mr Andrew Young, has been embraced several times in the past forty-eight hours'.

The magic name of Mossop echoed like a leak through the feast of spectres. All hands were called to the tiller as the Mixmasters came in on a wing and a prayer. Chants of 'Va Moose!' rose from the French quarters of the crowd. It was, however, not King Rex but the cricket reporter Brian Mossop (no usurpation) who answered the bugle of doom: 'He [Kim Hughes] might not be everybody's cup of tea, but let's hope he's given the chance to take the helm'.

The spectators were at a fever pitch on the tip of the iceberg as the Mixmasters drove on toward its climax. I asked a retired political commentator what he thought and he declared that the tournament would need a shot in the arm or it would be hoist on its own petard. 'The lancing of the boil must be the codpiece of any perceived scenario', he averred. A younger colleague agreed, adding that a catch-22 situation had been allowed to mushroom.

The last contestant stepped forward to dice with the trapdoor of fate. It was Ian Chappell who policed the cop-out of the night: 'Will the fire of McEnroe douse the ice man Borg?'

The sky was awash with the spectacle of two giant egg-beaters made from luminous silicon filled with helium. This was the signal that the judges had found a winner. I craned forward like a one-armed bill poster in a mad woman's jaccuzi. Who would it be?

Mr S.C.G. Hoodoo announced that Ian Chappell had bluffed and puckered his way to the pinnacle of the lake. Mr Chappell was ace number one, the baton-wielding supremo, the winner of the Grand Mixmasters Invitational, the top cocky in the bullring. As Mr Hoodoo spoke, the monsoon washed us all slowly out to sea.

As we struck out for Bali, I reflected on the organisation and presentation of the GMI. Perhaps it was time for a grass-roots reshuffle of the options open to the forward planners in the ivory think-tank of the pecking order.

25   The Last Tautology Pennant

*T*he 1983 Miracle Margarine $625 Australian Open Tautology Championships ('If it's a good tournament it's a Meadow Lea', said a Leagues' Club comedian) and the Allowrie Unsalted Butter $350 Grand Mixmasters Invitational (for Top People who Mix their Metaphors) held their historic first overlapping tournament at Kooyong last week.

The blending of these *grand prix* events was not without trauma, however. The immediate cause for the dovetailing was the flooding of Phuket Island off Thailand, where the Mixmasters had planned their event. 'Off-beat locale makes for interesting fare', said the television critics, but it was not to be. Now there were other problems in accommodating the sensitive Mixmasters with the rough-and-tumble world of tautology.

'I've got nothing against the Mixos', said a prominent leading tautologist, 'but that kind of pitty-pat stuff doesn't turn the public on'.

For their part, the Mixmasters were convinced that they were more subtle and international in their appeal than the parochial ockericity of the tautologists. 'Our tournaments have always been set overseas', sniffed a Mixmaster official, 'and it's only because Phuket Island was flooded that we've had to cut our cloth to hoist petards cheek by jowl with these awful taut- ologists'.

Be that as it may, the fans ignored the anti-dairy demon- strators and flocked to the big green bowl for this year's action. The tautologists kicked off under the grey Kooyong sky and right from the start the top seeds rumbled:

'I've watched the incident over and over again on videotape and I'm amazed that he was the only one singled out.'

— Rex Mossop, sports commentator

'It looks light enough to me, but I'm looking through my dark sunglasses.'

— Norman May, ABC TV

'He regards the "entombed" Parliament House as another example of Australia's cultural cringe, and its reliance on styles, vogues and cultural imagery imported from overseas.'

— Craig McGregor, *National Times*

'Here is a chance and opportunity to get totally involved in something completely new and fresh with none of the old ways to hinder progress.'

— Len Thompson, football columnist

'But in early television days I was certain of nothing. I had reverted to a novice, starting all over again.

— Geraldine Doogue, *Nationwide*

'He really took that tournament by storm, literally.'
> – Alan Stone, tennis commentator

It was a top game, top game. But while the Manly Rex wandered off to autograph copies of *Mossop's Foibles*, the heat went on:

'The worst thing that could happen is that the guest and I find each other mutually boring.'
> – Michael Parkinson, chat show host

'And undoubtedly, *We of the Never Never* is a spectacle for the eye.'
> – Anna-Maria Dell'Oso, film critic

'The players have found themselves competing against overhead planes departing from La Guardia airport.
> – Fred Stolle, tennis commentator

'This man who calls himself the Shadow Attorney-General is an academic, a lecturer, a theorist.'
> – Senator Carrick, Liberal, NSW

'The new prince is a baby boy.'
> – Terry Mabb, radio newsreader

'He has forever been immortalised as the handsome, womanising secret agent James Bond.'
> – Fantales biography of Sean Connery

Out in the middle they were aiming at the rib cage. But no one got fazed, not orators of this calibre:

'The Government should put more emphasis on our own indigenous research in this country.'
> – Chris Hurford, MHR

'Large free-standing classic mansion, *circa* around 1870, fully restored to its original splendour.'
> – Terrace House Factory ad

'John Moses concludes with his last paragraph.'

— Gillian Waite, 2ABC FM

'In his early years, Lyndon Johnson was a fawning sycophant.'

— *Time Magazine*

'Norths played well.'

— Ferris Ashton, *Sportsworld*

'A surprising number of Sydney people give a great deal of leisure time to amateur theatre as unpaid actors and behind-the-scenes production workers.'

— Margaret Smith, sociologist

The Mixmasters had been warming up on an outer court. Now they had a chance to strut their stuff and it was all Diadora, Tretorn, Fila and Tacchini for the next intermezzo, leaving Dunlop, Slazenger and Spalding in the shade.

'What to make of this slice of American pie, this pastoral adagio, this memoir-nightmare?'

— Richard Corliss, film critic

'I just went out like a log.'

— Sir William McMahon, millionaire

'Marian Street's opening innings under a new regime hung fire.'

— H.G. Kippax, theatre critic

'Young Turk of the corporate world, the braceletted and sometimes unbuttoned David Neate, has been a sword in the side of cobwebbed Melbourne furnishing company Kornblums ever since his share raid on the company in 1979.'

— Clancy, *National Times*

'If Newtown get the bone between their teeth, then Parramatta will be bridesmaids again.'

— Rex Mossop

'After a two-week break some teams are like rusty gates and fail to fire.'

– Rex Mossop

The big grey had run into a channel and gapped them. During the lunch-break the caterer was kept busy with orders of steak and beer for the tautologists and prosciutto and retsina for the Mixmasters. The President of the International Grand Prix Miracle Council was still negotiating hopefully for a possible outcome to the impasse when the tautologists took off their mouthguards and showed they had no truck with the coteries of officialdom.

'And a warning that Melbourne water supplies could be potentially dangerous.'

– David Johnston, ATV 10 News

'I just want to reiterate what I have stated and restated.'

– Alexander Haig, former US Secretary of State

'The film *Transmissions* written by Jeff Holland a Melbourne writer while living here, is described by the Producer as a 'Road, Rock, Quest, Thriller inspired by our unique scenery, and locations which exist nowhere else in the world" '

– Perth Institute of Film and TV

'I want all of the whole thing.'

– Laura Buzo, potential Christian

'Berri Estates Five Litres. 25 per cent more wine than a 4 litre cask.'

– Berri Estates wine cask label

'Dennis Lillee will be missed by whatever team he's not playing in.'

– Doug Walters, cricket legend

The Second Wave then left the Avant-garde behind with a breakthrough that established a new perspective.

'Donatien-Alphonse-François, Comte de Sade: sexual revolutionary or twisted pervert?'

– *National Times* Airwaves

'Lennox Walker forecasts Australia's future weather.'

– Women's Weekly

'I have discussed this matter with both Mr Fong Lim and Professor Clark and the true facts are that he did not speak to Sylvia and that he never went anywhere near the Press Club.'

– Cecil Black, Lord Mayor, Darwin

'Rape or sexual assault can occur at any stage to a person of any gender, male or female.'

– Dr Peter Bush, police surgeon

'Some scientists believe that the current flurry of cheating cases is nothing more than what they call an anomaly, a random quirk in the regular flow of events.'

– Time Magazine

'There's Farrah Fawcett and Ryan O'Neal — she remains lastingly beautiful, don't you agree?'

– Howard Cosell, American Mousse

It was Extra Special time and the following lifetime achievement awards were made to those who had distinguished themselves in their fields by their regular consistency over an epoch of legendary career-best aggregates.

Malaprop Handicap

King Rex took out the crown with what was widely acknowledged to be a Sheridanesque *non sequitur*:

'That wasn't Taylor, it was Sterling - I misconstrued him for Taylor.'

Inadequate Comma Sammy

This was quality fare by the *Herald* TV Guide when they previewed an episode of the *Mike Walsh Show*:

'Guests on the show will include the captains of the VFL Grand Final teams, Frank Thring and John Cain.'

Great New Class Screen Lovers Oscar

Jeremy Irons for *Brideshead Revisited*:

'I felt a bat-squeak of sexuality.'

The Doubles Cup

'This was a very close dead heat', explained Norman May.

Now let me explain what this means. You have to come up with an example of tautology *and* a mixed metaphor in the same session. I hope that's clear. Now the dead heat was a tight finish between Bill McLaren of BBC TV and Ray Martin of our own *Sixty Minutes* here at home. Now let's see who can take out this vocal derby.

'Welcome to Murrayfield which looks once more and not for the first time like an oasis of green in a sea of white.'
– Bill McLaren, BBC Rugby

'George has to carry the bachelor tag because he's single. It wouldn't be cricket if it was suggested that Ian and I were young blades around town.'
– Ray Martin, television reporter

Pelican Award

This prestigious prize to the Newspaper Placard Most Likely to Avoid a Libel Suit from a Quiz Compere went to the *Sun* for:

PAY RAID: MAN SHOT
IAN TURPIE AT HOME

After the mandatory commercial break, the Extra Special crowd were swept aside and it was tautology's turn. While the Mixmasters were eating quiche in the 'Invitation Only' marquee, the tautologists got into some slambang action out in the arena:

'It is still the reflex shots that are her [Cawley's] best - the unplanned, unpractised, unable to be practised, spur of the moment improvisations.'
— David Hickie, *National Times*

'There is also my favourite kind of audition, in which you may present material of your own choosing which you have prepared in advance.'
— Uta Hagen, actress

'Don't fill kerosene exceeding the capacity of the receptacle in order to avoid overflow.'
— Instructions for Moonlight hurricane lanterns

'Real names are not used in this fictional diary.'
— *Woman's Day*

'Now the gallery is finished the High Court gains from its close proximity.'
— Craig McGregor, *National Times*

'A man who scorns fashionable architectural vogues, dislikes grand-standing, and is little known outside his profession.'
— Craig McGregor

This boy McGregor was looking the goods and as much was acknowledged by former greats Norman May and Alan Stone, who withdrew from the tournament with grim smiles at the 'Craig Brigade'. But where was Rex Mossop? The veteran from Reef Beach, Balgowlah, who had triumphed so many times before, was not abroad on the rialto and some of his detractors got cocky. But I knew better.

The Moose was equally dangerous leading the field or charging. He always had a big following, rivalling the legendary 'Arnie's Army' that marched behind Arnold Palmer. 'Mossop's

Possums' were up in the trees, at every vantage point along the fairway when their man made his move.

' Someone has bodily manhandled Les Boyd.'

– Rex Mossop

'Kenny and Sterling, while not seen so much as a pair together, have been individually brilliant.'

– Rex Mossop

'The triple, yes, that's three consecutive tackles in succession.'

– Rex Mossop

It was top stuff, top stuff. The Remember Headingley Committee warned against over-confident complacency, but the Reefer was no dope. 'I'll deck these quincies', he averred.

'A particular welcome to Alan Clarkson and Geoff Gerard who have been in the studio there giving a little preamble before the start of this match.'

– Rex Mossop

'And he's got the *status quo* back to where it was.'

– Rex Mossop

'When Madigan discusses what he thinks architecture *should* be, words like "integrity" and "organic" and "nourishing" keep recurring.'

– Craig McGregor

The Craig Brigade was ecstatic. Their man was singled out and left on his own in the field they were calling Holocaust Hectares. But RM was not impressed. 'One more hoon to floor', rasped the Top Possum. It was the harsh voice of reality. No longer the preserve of gentlemen, tautology had become a financial business. The Moose was really rolling now:

'Edmondson kept his head against the wily experienced Ramirez in the crucial decider.'

'Well, do we say Cronulla was without Rogers? That's the old hackneyed chestnut, isn't it?'

'Difficult situation for a French referee to be in in this game because he's not an Englishman in terms of language; he talks his own home country language and can't converse with the players.'

It was all over. The 1983 Open went to the Miracle Piler Rex Mossop. The 31-year-old Golden Boy then announced his retirement before hopping into the royal box. Later, at a nastily convened press conference Rexlene said, 'I had a point to prove after that false start in Canberra in 1981, but now it's time to throw the chips in the towel bucket'.

The cleaners at Kooyong moved among rolling cans in the flapping sunset breeze. They knew as they looked up at the darkening sky of piebald amber and grey that they had seen the greatest of them all in his prime. And they were thankful. *Rexquiescat in pace.*

Children of Parody

26 All-comers Puff Contest

Brisbane: Friendly Giant to the North

*T*he history of Brisbane is a story of triumph over adversity, of progress, development, growth and expansion. In order to understand the Brisbane of today, it is necessary to spend a brief moment digesting the past. Brisbane was founded in 1824 by Lieutenant John Oxley, who brought with him some tourists from the UK. They all worked hard and made Brisbane what it is today.

The average Brisbanian is a friendly, cheerful soul, slow to anger and quick to make friends. Once you demonstrate that all you want to do is eat fresh mud crab at one of the city's 200 restaurants, then you will find that prices are reasonable and every second Thursday. The weather is often a talking point in Brisbane and it is generally warm in summer and cool in winter. The best time to visit the million-strong metropolis is from January to December. Unlike debt-plagued Argentina, public transport facilities are excellent, so you will have no trouble getting in and out.

A best-case scenario for a day in Brisbane is to start off with a stroll in the leaf-rich Botanic Gardens. Then have lunch at a tip-free bistro overlooking the river. You will be able to see where the mouth-watering mud crabs come from! For racing enthusiasts, nearby Eagle Farm is very definitely a must or, if you are more sedentarily inclined, a browse through one of Brisbane's shop-fringed malls will turn up a bargain or two. A night out in Brisbane is no longer a problem for visitors and for up-to-date information it is best to consult one of the city's colourful oath-using cabbies.

The economy of Brisbane is booming and everything is running smoothly. The city is clean and well governed. While you're there, remember that Brisbane was one of the allies in World War II and give them a salute. The average Brisbanian will appreciate any compliments you can offer and will be glad to hear you say it's fun to be part of the tourist boom. Happy snorkelling

27 Academia Awards

International Standards in Regional Aesthetics

*I*f one were to compare standards of criticism within and without national boundaries, one would be hard put to find a touchstone other than a case of plagiarism to make points of any consequence. No one work of art is so completely universal and so bereft of emotive bias that it can stand, incandescently, as the ultimate monument around which all wreaths may be judged equally. But in a case of plagiarism, all emotive bias to the work being reviewed is absent; the plagiarist has, essentially, no attitude to the work, and is thus able to reflect, objectively, regional differences.

The problem here is that there are not many plagiarists to whom one is able to turn for enlightenment. Most critics make up their own reviews; those who regurgitate what was said in the bar, use a pseudonym[1], or are unduly influenced by a spouse, a publicity officer, or a cheque, are not helpful to our quest because (a) no evidence of the original remains, and (b) all participants are of the same nationality.

How, then, are we to pursue our quest? Where are the plagiarists of the age? At this point, I should like to introduce the reader to Geraldine Pascall, critic of theatre and film for the *Australian*, a newspaper.

Now I do not suggest for a minute that Miss Pascall is a plagiarist. What I do suggest is that the conditions which we have found so ideal for our purpose in plagiarism are conditions which are to be found operating, intermittently but effectively, in the reviews of Miss Pascall.

Let us take an example from two reviews of the same play, *Equus* by Peter Shaffer. Michael Billington of the *Guardian*[2], London, wrote: 'Peter Shaffer's *Equus* fulfils a very ancient function of drama: it seeks to put dark, irrational forces that motivate much of our existence on to the stage . . . it works as an ecstatic conjuration of Dionysiac forces . . .'

Geraldine Pascall[3] wrote:

. . . it digs down into what drama was and still is about, fulfilling its most ancient function: trying to put on stage some of the dark, unknown, mysterious and irrational forces that can still frighten and move us . . . *Equus* works . . . because it so effectively conjures up these forces.

It is apparent that here we have two different approaches to the theatre, and, by extension, to art in general. Billington, the Englishman, is content to see tradition honoured. He says that the play 'fulfils a very ancient function of drama'. Immediately the reviewer has allotted a role for himself and for the artist. The reviewer has observed and is observing, and has matched the previous observation with the current observation. The reviewer thus occupies a role with no central dynamic; he is beyond the circle of creation or imaginative interpretation in both the perception of a phenomenon and in its dissemination. Peter Shaffer is similarly awarded the kudos reserved for one who reaffirms rather than challenges.

With Pascall, from a new society, the role of the reviewer is interpreted in a radically different way. Immediately she ascribes to herself a role which Billington does not assume. She adumbrates ('drama was') the phenomena of the past and redefines, creatively, the function of the contemporary manifestation of an admittedly ancient art ('and still is'). Nowhere in Billington do we find any inclination to venture beyond the traditional; but in Pascall we find an assertive opinion on the role of the drama today.

Similarly, Pascall ascribes to Shaffer a role which transcends the Billingtonian implication of passivity ('fulfils') and by its very nature ('digs down') gives Shaffer a function more in keeping with hardy inventive human beings such as pioneers, gold prospectors and investigative journalists. Shaffer, she asserts by her use of a suggestive transitive verb, is a dynamic innovator, not a role-playing traditionalist.

Finally, the passage shows us, with its inclusion on the one hand, and deletion on the other, of the term 'Dionysiac', the difference between one who is excessively given to find affirmation in the myths of the past and one who seeks to find new standards free from the inhibitive shibboleths of antiquity.

. . . the boy's intemperate passion for horses becomes a metaphor for any form of deviant love.

– Michael Billington

. . . The boy's intemperate passion for horses becomes a metaphor for any form of defiant love.

– Geraldine Pascall

Here we see no significant departure from the conditions necessary to assess differing standards of regional ideology; both reviewers demonstrate a similarity bordering on unanimity in the emotive bias towards the subject matter.

. . . the spectacle of the boy seeking to become one with the horses... only in the street outside do doubts about the argument begin.

– Michael Billington

. . . the boys [sic], for instance, seeking to become one with the horses . . . so that your own doubts don't really start to nag until you're out of the theatre.

– Geraldine Pascall

In these passages a valuable lesson about the extent and presence of subjectivity and objectivity — given, as we have established above, a reasonably similar response to the theme of the work — can be gleaned from the personal, intellectual response of the reviewer.

For Billington, the process of questioning inherited assumptions remains a consuetudinary procedure for society as a whole; it is even, he implies, a tradition in itself. Individual responsibility has not been relinquished to a collective ideology; it has never been entertained as an alternative in itself.

Pascall demonstrates with one phrase ('your own doubts') a vision of individual responsibility fused with observable phenomena as a vehicle for change within society as a whole. The proclivities towards subjectivity are certainly there; but they are harnessed to an evangelical desire to raise the level of objectivity both within and without the self.

It is cautionary, and proper, to add, however, that the uncanny resemblance between the phrases 'in the street outside' (Billington) and 'out of the theatre' (Pascall) shows a similarity that is a necessary counterweight to our evolving theories of cultural differences. Both reviewers, it is openly demonstrated, share a distrust for catharsis and a desire to extend the perception of drama beyond the walls of the playhouse.

He discovers that the child, with no music, art, friends or history to sustain him, finds in his worship of horses a substitute for religion and sex; and in the end he comes to question his right to eliminate that worship, however perverse a form it takes, and his duty to return the boy to our allegedly normal society ... Intellectually, one can pick all kinds of holes in the play's thesis. It argues the sanctity of worship and passion. But what if worship takes the form of racial intolerance?

– Michael Billington

Without education, art, history, skills or friends to sustain him, the boy has found in his worship of horses a substitute for religion and sex. And, in the end, Dysart doubts his right to take away that worship — however perverse, however much pain it causes the boy — and the value of returning him to normality ... But Shaffer's thesis relies on sanctifying worship and passion no matter what form it takes ...

– Geraldine Pascall

Here we have an accurate guide to the values of each of our participants, and, by extension, the values of the society they inhabit. The data extrapolation scale shows that these values have been placed in order by the reviewers themselves.

BILLINGTON	PASCALL
1. Music	1. Education
2. Art	2. Art
3. Friends	3. History
4. History	4. Skills
	5. Friends

For Billington, the old world has asserted itself over those ideas which could have been the harbingers of change in the theatre and on the street outside. That music and art should take precedence betrays a withdrawal from those areas in which the dynamics of revolution could viably fructify.

Pascall's thoughts reflect a more pragmatic, developing society, a society in which Education and Skills are paramount. But of all the evidence in this codification of the necessary, the most revealing is the credence given to 'Friends'. Billington places this at number three, whereas Pascall, displaying a rugged individualism not at odds with the pioneer spirit of her society, places 'Friends' last.

Alec McCowen's psychiatrist was remarkable for its questing intellectual hunger.

– Michael Billington

Dysart should have more dimension — a hungry questing intelligence ...

– Geraldine Pascall

The definition of attitudes towards the solution to the perennial question 'What is Man?' and its corollary 'What does Man want?' has never been more clearly focussed. Billington withdraws into the effete notion of 'intellectual hunger' and envisages, even proselytises for, a world of civilised intercourse among the intelligentsia.

The instinctive lapse into elitism which characterises Billington's ideological drawbridge is triumphantly undermined by Pascall's pensive reversal. The 'questing intelligence' she unleashes is clearly directed towards a continuing, relevant Cultural Revolution that aims to reform in and out of the theatre.

It is one thing, however, to animadvert to the point of invective on the inadequacy of an old society *vis-à-vis* a new one; it is quite another to indulge in deviant metaphor by hurling into the literary ring two bantams from frontier societies at the interface of the hemispheres. Some similarities on the following comparisons must be made immediately.

Both reviewers, Geraldine Pascall and the American John Skow of *Time* magazine, have seen the same film, *The Duellists*. Consider their differing reactions to the film's opening:

We understand immediately ... Duels at dawn are as familiar as gravesides in the rain.

– John Skow[4]

There have been many movies . . . that have begun with or used duels at dawn. We recognise the signals and we know the rites to come.

– Geraldine Pascall[5]

Here we see only a cursory nod to tradition and even here, tradition is downgraded to the status of cliché. From the very beginning, Skow and Pascall are searching for new horizons, as their forebears did before them.

Several hundred films have used ground fog rising off fields and the dark figures of waiting men to give the same contrast between soft landscape and hard purpose.

– John Skow

the soft, welcoming beauty of the landscape is an immediate contrast to the savagery of the men who use it.

– Geraldine Pascall

The essence of Pascall lies once again in the pragmatic thrust of the argument. While Skow generalises about 'hard purpose' (what purpose? who is hard?), Pascall defines the violation of land by the 'men who use it'. Concern for the dimensions and caparison of the figures in the landscape can be traced to Pascall's humanity as contrasted with Skow's fundamentally American impersonality.

... a young hussar lieutenant named D'Hubert (Keith Carradine), an unexceptional man, collides with another lieutenant named Feraud (Harvey Keitel). Feraud is a strutting, bloody-minded fool, and he challenges D'Hubert to a duel. Though D'Hubert knows that the matter is silly, honor forces him to fight. Feraud is wounded ...

– John Skow

D'Hubert (Keith Carradine), a young hussar lieutenant and a fairly ordinary man, unintentionally upsets another lieutenant, Feraud (Harvey Keitel), a pompous, arrogant fanatic, and Feraud challenges him to a duel. D'Hubert realises the cause is foolish and the means to settle it unnecessary but his own code of honor [sic] requires that he fight. He wounds Feraud ...

– Geraldine Pascall

The key here is that Skow finds D'Hubert (Keith Carradine) 'unexceptional' whereas Pascall's description, 'fairly ordinary', emphasises the extremes of empathy to be found at either end of the Pacific.

Because D'Hubert (Keith Carradine) has not Rockefellered his way to immortality by building a railroad or dying in the saddle, he is, perforce, 'unexceptional'. The warmth and compassion of Pascall for the battler, the underdog, the person in the street has never before been demonstrated to greater effect.

Feraud remains crazed with hatred, and D'Hubert, though he cannot remember the original cause of the quarrel and is quite willing to forget the feud, continues to dance to honor's tune and his adversary's whim. Though Feraud's mania never subsides, and though D'Hubert thinks him contemptible, the two are bound together in something that is almost comradeship.

– John Skow

Though both no longer remember the original cause of the quarrel, Feraud's frenzy continues and D'Hubert must march to the same drum.

In the end the mad grandeur of their actions creates a sort of bond between them ...

– Geraldine Pascall

The internal decline of America, limned by de Tocqueville with effortless prescience, has yet to find a more rewarding proponent that John Skow. To show Skow's 'tune' parallelled, boarded and sunk by the omniscient gunboat rodomontade of Pascall's 'drum' is to see a ferris wheel baying at a helicopter. The gesture is inadequate, even fraudulent, and must perforce foreshadow a questioning of values and a redefinition of what constitutes, if in fact it ever did, the 'new world' or indeed, for that matter, the 'brave new world', for the gulf of conceptualising has narrowed to the point of necromantic purification.

Given the difficulty of obtaining suitable role-models to enable comparisons to be made on the level of plagiarism, it is nevertheless of inestimable value to be able to draw conclusions between those values propagated in the northern hemisphere by Michael Billington and John Skow, and those crusaded for in the southern hemisphere by Geraldine Pascall, whose critical pantheon has always placed a high honour on writers of rigorous originality.[6]

While the ultimate conditions for assessing regional aesthetics and their consequent prognostications for the idiosyncrasies of their societies must wait until a foreign reviewer 'goes all the way' and plagiarises Geraldine Pascall, we can nevertheless make a beginning by observing those confluences where the seeds of such interaction have already begun fruitfully to interweave.

Footnotes

1 E.g. V.I. Richards, the Melbourne critic of *Theatre Australia*, is a pseudonym for Roy Fredericks.
2 *The Guardian*, 21 April 1976, quoted in *Theatre Australia*, Oct/Nov 1976.
3 *The Australian*, 28 September 1976, quoted in *Theatre Australia*, *op cit.*
4 *Time*, 6 February 1978.
5 *The Australian*, 4–5 February 1978.
6 *Time* is published on the Wednesday five days before the issue date. *Time* of 6 February 1978 was therefore published on 1 February 1978.

28 Time, After Time

Gibson. Coach.

Balding, charismatic Jack Gibson, his rock-like jaw jutting at a military angle, started in football as a workaday prop tasking for Easts and Wests. Then, shrewdly crystal-balling the post-permissive era that began in 1967, Gibson took a flock of raw rookies and seasoned veterans and melded them into an eastside unit that cauterised all opponents and ballooned rapidly into a footballing *cause célèbre*. 'Gibbo tackled us out of the running', said a rival coach ruefully. 'This was top-hole stuff', observed a British attaché. Then it all began to go wrong for Big Jack. Filibustering officials sank in the knife and Gibson found himself in the wilderness. The girth became flaccid. The eyes lost their gimlet veracity. 'I saw him grow old in a chair', says a friend. During the years that followed, Gibson chopped wood on his farm and bided his time. 'I knew he was only biding his time', said a disgruntled turkey, voicing valid concerns of a pre-Christmas era. Then, with his new-found strength, Gibson opted boldly to return to the fray. The glory years of '74 and '75 saw a refurbished Easts sweep the board. Gibson, 49, earned $1.5 million in the fiscal year. Midst laurels stood the Rip Kirby look-alike, who was given the freedom of New York by a grateful mayor. 'Jack was at his zenith', allows a friendly foe. 'Gibson was the chief ass-kicker on the block', argues an American aide from a pro-Republican southern state. Staring out at the sea from his Fullersome bayside villa-dome, Jack Gibson knew he was home. But then came disaster. Easts lost to a refurbished Canterbury in a '76 semi and a pre-permissive era had ended. The Gibsonorous phrases like 'tackle count' and 'shut-out' fell from grace. Soon Gibson was begging for handouts on skid row. 'He was one of us', commented a hard-bitten derelict. 'I lika da spaghetti', confessed an Italian glutton. 'I'll be back', promised Gibson. And he was. To do battle with the Ryanamics of a refurbished Newtown side and give them the Raudonikiss of death. Once again, the Gibsonomes were Pollyannaish. It was glory, glory, glory all through the early eighties as the Parramatta Eels, until then relative unknowns, put together three premierships back to back. Despite cutbacks (estimated at $1.6 million in 1984) in rugby league's carrot v. stick economic hegemony, Gibson retained a measure of autonomy. Said Swinburne B.J. Wong, director of the International Pacific Studies Program at the Chinese University of Hong Kong: '[Parramatta's] President Dennis Fitzgerald has exercised [his] rights in a flexible and pragmatic way. The days of negative growth are [over]'. In a move that surprised Fitzgerald, 52, the free-basing Gibson took charge of the ageing Cronulla Sharks. In long-sought talks the League ended the brief thaw by sacking the revenue-poor southerners. Some analysts voiced the view that Gibson was finished, but an astonishing 34.7 per cent of North Sydney fans believed that 'Gibbo was coming', whereas other key observers runed that colourful medical entrepreneur Dr Geoffrey Edelsten would mount a helm-taking merger raid (the flamboyant medico, 51, proposed that the Sharks swim under his umbrella in a user-friendly income hike). Whether he triggers off this last-ditch ploy or mounts a crackdown on career-change rumours, one thing is certain: Jack Gibson has waged an all-out assault on the it-can't-be-done brigade.

– compiled by Talbot E. Rosenblatt from reports by P.J. Foxglove Biltmore and Beverley Grimaldi Vandenberg

Satire Limits

At the climax of *Big River* the heroine cries out in anguish, 'I've failed in my life, I've failed'. I knew exactly how she felt when I heard Senator Fred Chaney say, 'History is behind us and the future is ahead of us'. Senator Chaney was speaking of the replacement of Andrew Peacock as Liberal leader by John Howard, but my anguish was not caused by any irredeemable commitment to the Peacock cause. What upset me was that Senator Chaney had uttered a whopper of a tautology and I had thought this linguistic sin was on the way out because of my satirical writings on the subject.

In fact, tautology is alive and well, thanks to the efforts of sports commentators like Darrell Eastlake, whose most recent gem was 'He's having a great début first up'. Theatre critic Bob Evans described a character in a play as 'an unknown stranger'. Even the comparative tranquillity of the Pioneer cassette car stereo manual is disturbed by this kind of thing: 'Car stereo operation should be performed while a car stops. For safety driving, be sure to operate the car stereo while your car stops. Otherwise you may come across an unexpected accident'. Sophisticated listeners will recognise the signs of translation from the Japanese in that extract and realise that we are dealing with a multinational concern. Even further afield, BBC cricket commentator Brian Johnston brought an English flavour to tautology. According to Nancy Mitford, it is U to say spectacles and non-U to say glasses. Brian Johnston embodied the indigenous obsession with social class when he described Murray Bennett as 'a bespectacled bowler wearing dark glasses'. In another exotic land, North Queensland, a single, lonely and apparently troppo cane farmer advertised for a 'female girl or lass' to keep him company. Perhaps he lived near the waterway north of Townsville which is called 'Black Gin Creek'.

One time at a reception a South Australian sidled up to me. 'You know of course about the rumour-mill in Adelaide', he whispered confidentially. This predisposition towards tautology without actually committing it is not confined to the Athens of the South. A positive swab has been returned from the sometime president of the Queensland Rugby League, Senator Ron McAuliffe. When a prominent local footballer, Chris Phelan, received an offer from 'down south', Senator Ron intervened. He said he had established an Outstanding Players Retention Fund to keep Phelan and his ilk in the north. Nevertheless, Phelan subsequently went to Sydney for a $40,000 transfer fee. Was McAuliffe irked by this? Not a bit of it. He professed to be overjoyed. 'This $40,000 will be a tremendous boost for our Outstanding Players Retention Fund', he said.

Quango man Phillip Adams counselled patience to those who are getting exasperated with the Commission for the Future's lack of progress. In another twelve months, he says, the organisation will be really hitting its straps. Science Minister Barry Jones confesses to some impatience for results, but realistically, he says, the commission must be given two to three years. (All of which points to the ineffectiveness of another quango, the Sludge Abatement Board.)

This process of institutionalising tautology can also be seen in currently prevalent clichés, such as 'digs beneath the surface', 'going round in circles', 'we'll send you a free gift', 'no previous experience necessary', 'there's no one in that gap' and 'added bonus'. The NSW Institute of Tautology, Rex Mossop, kept up appearances with a description of footballer Mario Fenech ('He's a very good-looking handsome young man') while rock writer Tim Toni seemed to speak for a new generation when he stated, 'The Lighthouse Keepers is disbanding after tonight's farewell gig at the Graphic Arts Club'.

Sometimes people ask me how effective satire is. 'Not at all', I say.

Notes on Contributions

1 There was pandemonium at a book reading at my school when we were told 'There was a bed of sorts in the corner'. The entertainers whose catch-phrases are quoted are: Roy Rene, Jackie Gleason, Joe Sandow, Muhammad Ali, Jack Davey, Gough Whitlam, Jack Lord, Bob Rogers, ET, John Cleese, Don Adams, Ward 'Pally' Austin, Ian 'Molly' Meldrum, Don Lane.

2 Kenneth Tynan's witty, liberating reviews graced the fifties and sixties. He faltered during the ordeal that was the seventies and died in California of emphysema in 1980. Tynan was the supreme stylist who *never* used terms like 'phallic symbol', 'very unique', 'cunning stunts' or 'heroic pooch'. One of my precis treasures is this description from a TV guide: 12.00 Jet Over the Atlantic (PGR,59,b/w). Drama about an explosion on an aircraft. George Raft.

No doubt if he were asked if kidney was offal, Tony Travert would say only if it were cooked so much it got scotched.

7 The New Class had had a pretty good innings but by the mid eighties the psychic epidemic was all but over.

9 The answers to the Quick Quiz are 1 (a) and 2 (d).

13 The Netertainment Guide is not alone. The *Sun-Herald* advertised *Creator*, starring Peter O'Tootle.

16 Lauries Meatland had no apostrophe. Maybe they thought it was the cow's.

21 Social cricket club secretaries are used to finding all sorts of phone messages on the pad, such as John Crane is painting in Otford this weekend or Greg Haddrick has moved to *A Country Practice* and has to finish his script by Monday. The most poignant, almost unbearable in its moving simplicity, was Sarah de Jong can't score tomorrow.

23 Supporting the North Sydney rugby league team (last premiership: 1922) is very much 'the love that dare not speak its name'. Over the years demented fans have changed the 'Norths to Win' sign to 'Norths to Score', contemplated migrating to Ulan Bator, and sent the administrators' names (Norths' officials are known as the 1922 Committee) to Exit, the voluntary euthanasia society.

24 The last picture show seen by the contestants on the eve of the event was a motivational film called *Red River*, in which John Wayne declares, 'I don't like quitters, especially when they can't finish what they start.'

26 Some people take violent exception to what some writers write. The concept of the writer as someone who may see things differently or pose awkward questions is beyond them. They just want puffs. I have met some of these good folk who do not believe that it is the writer's role to question the conventional wisdom. This puff is for them.

27 This satire on academic prose appeared in *Linq* in 1979. It acquired an 'underground' reputation.

29 Alexander Haig returned to the land of the alive and living with 'The only way that the Republican Party can hold the White House in 1988 is to nominate a candidate who can win'. Theatre critic Michael Morton-Evans proved he was worth his weight with 'As played by Rhonda Wilson, Isabella has to be one of the most compelling female heroines since Molly Bloom', while Rex Mossop could have been describing himself when he said, 'You've been a crowd-pleaser to a lot of people'.